D1743895

The Book of Revelation
from *A* to *Z*

The Book of Revelation

from  to

THEMES, TOPICS, TERMS, SYMBOLIC WORDS AND VOCABULARY

FROM THE BOOK OF REVELATION

Compiled by Clay A. Westover

Springville, Utah

Copyright © 2004 Clay A. Westover

All Rights Reserved.

No part of this book may be reproduced in any form whatsoever, whether by graphic, visual, electronic, film, microfilm, tape recording, or any other means, without prior written permission of the author, except in the case of brief passages embodied in critical reviews and articles.

ISBN: 1-55517-738-7
e.1

Published by CFI
An imprint of Cedar Fort Inc.
www.cedarfort.com

Distributed by:

Cover design by Nicole Cunningham
Cover design © 2003 by Lyle Mortimer

Printed in the United States of America
10 9 8 7 6 5 4 3 2 1

Printed on acid-free paper

Library of Congress Control Number: 2003116467

Introduction to
John's Book of Revelation

The book of Revelation is also known as the "Apocalypse." What does "Apocalypse" mean?

What is John "unveiling" or "revealing?" If the book of Revelation is John's "unveiling" of Jesus Christ in His fullness of glory and majesty, why do not the Saints spend more time studying this powerful testimony of an Apostle known as the Lord's "beloved?"

Why are images of chaos and destruction so often associated with John's Revelation, rather than the oft-mentioned blessings and positive concepts taught in this remarkable book?

What can we do to tackle the difficult problem of symbolism, imagery, prophetic speech patterns and metaphorical comparisons in unraveling the writings of John the Revelator?

Is There Hope?

According to eminent gospel scholar and professor of religion Gerald Lund, a member the Quorum of Seventy, and the late Elder Bruce R. McConkie, a member of the Quorum of the Twelve Apostles, it is very difficult to read the "prophetic writings," which constitute a significant portion of the standard works, without immediately confronting language that is rich in symbolism, culture, comparison and contrasts, imagery, figurative expressions, allegories and parables. Many Latter-day Saints fail to understand or ignore the prophetic writings contained in our arsenal of Holy Writ basically for the same reason that King Noah and his Priests did not understand them. "Ye have not applied your hearts to understanding; therefore, Ye have not been wise." Abinadi's indictment is as much applicable today as it was then: "Therefore, what teach ye this people?" (Mosiah 12:27). Abinadi adds: "I perceive that they [the commandments] are not written in your hearts" (Mosiah 13:11). We are easily overwhelmed or fatigued when forced to deal with such concepts as types, shadows, similitude/similes, metaphors, complex literary styles and poetry, patterns and prefiguration. More than 25 percent of our scriptural texts are prophetic in nature, that is, they are not history, law, commandments, genealogies, explanations, instructions or discourses. The prophetic writings, including the Psalms (Luke 24:27,44), are meant to be understood by the Latter-day Saints. First, Jacob prophesied that "none of the prophets have written, nor prophesied, save they have spoken concerning this Christ" (Jacob 7:11; 4:4-6). To have a testimony of Jesus Christ is the "spirit of prophecy" (Rev. 19:10). This same "spirit" enlightens the mind and brings understanding. Second, the prophets themselves said their prophecies were written to be understood by those living in the last days (Jeremiah 23:20; Isaiah 29:23-24; DNTC, p. 431).

Elder McConkie assures us that understanding is possible "if we apply ourselves with full purpose of heart. The language and imagery is so chosen as to appeal to the maturing gospel scholar, to those that already love the Lord and have some knowledge of his goodness and grace" (Ensign, Sept. 1975). We are living in exciting times when we may be witnesses to the "things which must shortly come to pass" (Rev. 1:1). There will be trials and tribulations, but unlike our ancestors who have gone before us, we will emerge from the darkness and the refiner's fire into a new day, the dawning of the millennial reign when "God shall wipe away all tears from [our] eyes; and there shall be no more death, neither sorrow, nor crying, neither shall there be any more pain; for the former things are passed away" (Rev. 21:4). The Prophet Joseph Smith reminds us of great promises when we receive God's seal and election (Rev. 7:3), and when the judgments come upon the world we will recognize them for what they are and the assurance of deliverance is "an anchor to the soul, sure and steadfast. Though the thunders might roll and lightnings flash, and earthquakes bellow, and war gather thick around, yet this hope and knowledge would support the soul in every hour of trial, trouble and tribulation" (TPJS, p. 298).

Joseph Smith taught that "John had the curtains of heaven withdrawn, and by vision looked through the dark vista of future ages, and contemplated events that should transpire throughout every subsequent period of time, until the final winding up scene." What follows this introduction is a glossary of terms, phrases, symbols and vocabulary found in the book of Revelation. The various definitions and explanations are suggestions only to help interested persons that "readeth, and that hear the words of this prophecy, and keep those things which are written therein: for the time is at hand" (Rev. 1:3).

The following abbreviations appear in this work:

CR – Conference Report
DNTC – Doctrinal New Testament Commentary
HC – History of the Church
JD – Journal of Discourses
JST – Joseph Smith Translation
TPJS – Teachings of the Prophet Joseph Smith
YWJ – Young Women's Journal

The Book of Revelation:
$\mathcal{A}$ - $\mathcal{Z}$

GLOSSARY OF TERMS AND PHRASES

[A Vocabulary Guide to Reading the Book of Revelation]

Preface

The compiler of this glossary of terms and phrases used in the book of Revelation is a student of the scriptures, loves to teach and talk about the doctrines and teachings of the Lord, and endeavors to be a follower of the Master Jesus Christ. He's had the occasion to ask members of Sunday School classes and other groups the meaning of the word "Apocalypse." Most respond with words such as catastrophe, disaster, cataclysm, etc,. Apocalypse, the Greek name for revelation, means "the unveiling." What is it that is being unveiled, or revealed, in the Apocalypse? It is that God, through His Son, controls the forces governing the universe and that good will ultimately triumph over evil. In spite of being one of the most clear and inspired books in the Bible, the Apocalypse has been the subject of endless hype and speculation, as evidenced by the numerous fictional works and movies on the subject. The world is not doomed to be destroyed in the holocaust of atomic warfare and a nuclear winter. It is truly sad that so many remain "fearful and unbelieving" (Rev. 21:8).

According to John's revelation this very earth is to be exalted and glorified and become the dwelling place of God and the righteous saints (Rev. 21:1-3; D&C 88:25-26). Furthermore, the Lord, through His Apostle John, pronounces wonderful blessings upon those who "overcome" the world. These beatitudes are repeated throughout the book of Revelation. We would do well to review the Lord's word given through the Prophet Joseph: "Look unto me in every thought; doubt not, fear not" (D&C 6:36).

Many definitive and authoritative books and articles have been written about the Apocalypse. However, only the most serious student of the Bible will go to church carrying a box of Bible dictionaries and commentaries. Most church-goers seem to be content to listen to their respective clergy and teachers interpret Bible passages for them. Unfortunately, this attitude deprives individuals of the joy that is derived from personally examining the holy writ, reading it page by page, verse by verse, and word by word. It is for this purpose that this author conceived of the idea of breaking from the commentary format in favor of an alphabetical listing of words, terms, symbols and phrases to provide the reader with references, definitions and interpretations as appropriate. Advice given by Elder Bruce R. McConkie is appropriate in this regard: "Read, ponder, and pray—verse by verse, thought by thought, passage by passage, chapter by chapter!" (Ensign, Oct. 1973, p.83).

The glossary entries are suggested interpretations only. Content is based on sources such as Bible dictionaries, scriptural footnotes and cross-references, computer-aided word studies and commentaries of Biblical scholars. This glossary is designed as an aid to help guide students of the Bible in their studies of the prophetic writings of John and the book of Revelation. This compilation has deliberately been kept short and definitions concise and compact in order to make this work both portable and practical. The listing of vocabulary, terms and phrases is lengthy enough to be interesting and informative and at the same time small enough to fit into the reader's notebook or folder. Each entry in the glossary contains its reference in Revelation and many entries are cross-referenced to other books of scripture. Where several interpretations are possible for a glossary entry, each explanation is separated from another by a semi-colon. The reader should keep in mind that passages in Revelation may be understood at different levels; literal or figurative, physical or spiritual, etc. Therefore, the few explanations for one entry are not necessarily mutually exclusive. Effort has been made to construct the defining of words, symbols and phrases in such a way as to not constitute an endorsement or favor any narrow religious, political or social viewpoint.

It is the heartfelt desire of this writer that the reader, with glossary in hand, will feel inspired and challenged to fearlessly delve into the book of Revelation and experience the same inner awakening and spiritual uplift that was experienced by the compiler of this glossary. Professor Victor L. Ludlow gives the following valuable counsel: "Spiritual growth is a gradual learning process that requires constant effort . . . because of its complicated nature and because of its elusiveness in a temporal world" (Isaiah: Prophet,

Seer, and Poet, p. 260).

The Apocalypse represents a message of comfort and hope to all who believe in the redeeming power of Jesus Christ and to all who echo the words of John, "Even so, come, Lord Jesus" (Rev. 22:20). Never before has the message of the Apocalypse been more relevant and compelling than now.

THEMES, TOPICS, TERMS, SYMBOLIC WORDS, AND VOCABULARY

FROM THE BOOK OF REVELATION

-C𝒜-

ABADDON [Hebrew for ruin]/APOLLYON [Greek for destroyer — (Rev. 9:11) Angel of the Abyss. Interpreted as being Lucifer/Satan.

ABOMINATION[S] — (Rev. 17:4; 21:27) That which is detestable, repulsive or offensive to God.

ABYSS – (Rev. 9:11; 17:8; 20:1-3) Bottomless pit; Dwelling place and, ironically, the final resting place for Satan, the beast, and the false prophet; Often used as synonym for hell, hades, Sheol; Place of confinement.

ACCORDING TO [HIS] WORKS – (Rev. 2:23) *See* **Works, According to.**

ACCUSER – (Rev. 12:10) Another name for Satan that comes from the Greek word for devil and means false accuser, slanderer, faultfinder. The devil's role as accuser stands in stark contrast to Jesus' role as our advocate "for He lives to make intercession" (Heb. 7:25).

ADMIRATION – (Rev. 17:6) Amazement, astonishment.

ADULTERY – (JST Rev. 2:20,22) Grave sin of sexual immorality that not only involves illicit conduct with another, but entails a turning away from a covenant relationship with another; Apostasy, rejection of the truth.

AFFLICTIONS/ADVERSITY – (Rev. 6:12-13; 8:7-13; 16:1-16) (Psalms 34:19; Isaiah 30:20; 48:10; 1 Peter 4:12-13; D&C 45:26,33,40-42; 88:87; JS-Matt. 1:29,32-33) Things suffered in mortality—such as persecution, hurt, disease, woes, plagues, sun, heat, wind, thirst and hunger—are to be interpreted both as literal [suffered physically in mortality] and symbolic [representative of a spiritual reality] as types of tribulations or curses from God. Tribulations, afflictions and adversities are to prompt men to remember God and repent (Rev. 9:20-21; 16:9,11), learn patience [*See* **Endure well to the end**], serve others who are in greater need than themselves, and put their lives in order through setting proper priorities. If we fail to set proper goals, God in His wisdom may see fit to tutor us with "opportunities," as Brigham Young called them. The basic message of the book of Revelation is that the world is NOT destined to a nuclear demise having succumbed to war and tribulation, but the earth is to be redeemed and glorified.

AGATE – (Rev. 21:19) Translucent [semi-transparent] crystallized quartz; Alternate translation for chalcedony (Ex. 28:19). Precious stone included on the breastplate of the high priest.

AGENCY/FREE WILL – (Rev. 12:4) (2 Nephi 2:27; 10:23; Abr. 3:27-28; D&C 29:35) Prior to the creation of this earth and our mortal lives, fully one-third of all the hosts who contemplated the challenges of mortal life allowed themselves to be deluded into thinking that there were acceptable alternatives to the risks that accompany the exercise of agency and free will under conditions that would prevail upon earth. They chose to follow Satan, lost their opportunity to be born into mortality, and continue to influence mortals in their decisions and exercise of free will. Agency was and is a gift from God. "And now remember, remember, my brethren, that whosoever perisheth, perisheth unto himself; and whosoever doeth iniquity, doeth it unto himself; for behold ye are free; ye are permitted to act for yourselves; for behold, God hath given unto you a knowledge and he hath made you free" (Helaman 14:30).

ALAS – (Rev. 18:16,19) Exclamation of concern and unhappiness over loss or misfortune.

ALLELUIA – (Rev. 19:1,4,6) Greek rendition of the phrase "Jehovah be praised."

ALMIGHTY/OMNIPOTENT – (Rev. 1:8; 4:8; 11:17; 15:3; 16:14; 19:6,15; 21:22) (Gen. 17:1; Ex. 6:3; Psalms 91:1; 2 Cor. 6:18) All powerful; Superlative attribute of God and His Son, implying there is no power greater than theirs. Theirs is the power to sustain, support, deliver and preserve their children.

ALPHA AND OMEGA – "The first and the last;" Name of Jesus which indicates the eternal nature of His life, mission and destiny (Rev. 1:8,11; 21:6; 22:13) (D&C 19:1; D&C 38:1; D&C 45:7).

ALTAR – (Rev. 6:9; 8:3-5; 9:13; 14:18; 16:7) An image associated with sacrifice and with God's judgment.

From Revelation we know that there is an altar in heaven where fragrant incense of prayer and worship ascend to the Father.

AMEN – (Rev. 7:12; 19:4) Expression of agreement, acceptance by a witness as to truth or validity of something; (Num. 5:22) The word 'Amen' attributes to Jesus Christ the characteristics of being sure, true, trustworthy; Divine affirmation (*See* Mormon Doctrine, p. 32).

AMEN, THE – (Rev. 3:14) Jesus Christ (Isaiah 65:16— God of Amen); the Truth.

AMETHYST – Gemstone of crystallized quartz that varies in color from pale-blue to a deep purple color; Symbol of royal priesthood; (Ex. 28:19; 39:12) Included in breastplate of the high priest; (Rev. 21:20) Twelfth stone included in the foundation of the wall of the New Jerusalem.

ANGEL [Another, Mighty, Seventh, Strong] – Michael. (Rev. 5:2; 7:2; 8:3; 10:1; 11:15; 14:6,15; 18:1,21) (Dan. 12:1; D&C 88:92,105-106,112; 133:36-40) "Another angel" may be a composite representation symbolic of all the heavenly beings who participated, or will participate in the Restoration of the gospel and establishment of the Lord's Kingdom (Bruce R. McConkie, DNTC, 3:492,530). Some commentators go as far as to say that possibly John himself is 'another angel' since his mission of the Restoration and testimony continues (Rev. 10:11). John is to play a prominent role in the effort to "gather the tribes of Israel" (D&C 77:14); Finally, the last and most speculative interpretation as to who 'another angel' is, whose voice is heard above all others, and whom John sees [but is not one of the seven angels, and not one of the four angels] is the presiding priesthood officer who holds the keys of the era or dispensation being observed in the vision.This means that the angel that is instructing the other angels as they sound the trumpets and pour the vials of God's condemnation upon the earth may be Joseph Smith, the founding prophet of this dispensation, or it may be the prophet and president of the Church of Jesus Christ of Latter-day Saints who is in office and holds the keys at the time of tribulation. There is a key doctrine of the Second Coming that involves the appearance of our first father Adam [Michael, as we know him in modern scripture, and the angel being discussed herein] and Jesus Christ at Adam-ondi-Ahman at some point in time before Christ's coming in glory for the whole world to witness (Dan. 7:9-10; D&C Sections 107 and 116; The Millennial Messiah, Bruce R. McConkie, pp. 578-588). At that time all priesthood holders, past and present, who have held the keys of the priesthood will attend a gathering with Adam and the Son of God. There they will give an accounting of their stewardships and return the keys to their rightful owner, Jesus Christ. It is believed that it is here that the final judgement begins and the righteous priesthood holders and others will receive their crowns of glory (Rev. 20:4). At that assembly the Messiah, according to His wisdom, will direct the affairs of the Kingdom in order to preserve His fold and usher in His personal reign upon the earth. John in his Revelation has been generous in interpreting his own writings at times. At other times, the identities of persons and events are left veiled or ambiguous, making any logical reasoning and speculation in vain, due to the fact that we live in a very changeable world experiencing unpredictable conditions. We mortals, without divine revelation, are not very good at understanding the mind and will of God (Isaiah 55:8-9).

ANGEL, AS FLAMING FIRE AND A MINISTERING ANGEL – (D&C 7:6) John the Revelator.

ANGEL ASCENDING FROM THE EAST – (Rev. 7:2) (D&C 77:9) An Elias come from the presence of God to help in the gathering of the children of Israel prior to the punishing scourges that will encompass the earth before the Second Coming.

ANGELS – (Rev. 3:5; 5:11; 7:11) (D&C 77:12) God's heavenly messengers (Heb. 1); (Rev. 1:1; 22:16) Witnesses in heaven; Mortal servants [of God] with a divinely appointed errand, God's agents who execute His will and judgments upon the world; Fellowservants. (Rev. 19:10; 22:6,8-9,16) (D&C 129) President Joseph F. Smith clarified who and what angels are: "We are told by the Prophet Joseph Smith that 'there are no angels who minister to this earth but those who do belong or have belonged to it.' Hence, when messengers are sent to minister to the inhabitants of the earth, they are not strangers, but from the ranks of our kindred, friends, and fellow-beings and fellow-servants" (Gospel Doctrine, p. 435).

ANGEL[S] OF THE BOTTOMLESS PIT – (Rev. 9:11) Satan; Demonic angels of the devil.

ANGER – *See* **Wrath.**

ANTICHRISTS/ FALSE TEACHERS/ FALSE PROPHETS – (Rev. 2:2) (Isaiah 29:9-10; Micah 3:6-7; 2 Cor. 11:13-14; Titus 1:10-11; 1 John 2:18,22; 4:1,3; 2 John 1:7; 2 Nephi 28:12; D&C 64:38-39) *See* **Apostasy;** The appearance of false teachers among the saints has been a common phenomenon throughout the history of the world, but John the Revelator makes mention of a particular anti-Christ that will arise in the last days who will be especially powerful and convincing (Rev. 13:11-13; 16:13; 19:20; 20:10) (2 Thess. 2:9); Even if we interpret John's description of the anti-Christ literally, that such a person will appear in the flesh, this person serves as a type or pattern of the many false, vain, covetous and lying teachers that will cover the earth in the last days (2 Peter 2:1-3,12-20; 3:1-3). There are sure signs and key features by which one might know and distinguish between the "teacher come from God" (John 3:2) and false prophets.

The true and inspired teacher is characterized by the following:

Teaches the doctrines of Jesus Christ by the power of the Holy Ghost because he loves the Lord and those he teaches.

Loves knowledge and loves that which is good, is able to discern between good and evil, and distinguish between what is important in terms of doctrine and what is not (Jeremiah 3:15).

Gains knowledge, teaching skill and abilities at his own expense in terms of time, effort and money, and is NOT part of a paid ministry or professionally educated class or clergy (Jeremiah 9:3,8; 10:21).

Teaches by the power of and/or under the direction of the true priesthood of God.

Teaches that which is harmonious with the scriptures, consistent with the practices of living a good moral and ethical life (Thirteenth Article of Faith), and consistent with the words of other inspired teachers; that is, he is particularly in tune with the words of modern day Apostles and Prophets.

The instruction and the memory of inspired teachers will remain with attentive and diligent class members and students who listen with prepared minds and with willing and meek spirits. The effects of good teaching will be reflected in the lives and conduct of the students (Isaiah 30:20-21).

ANTIPAS – (Rev. 2:13) According to tradition, Antipas was a faithful saint of Pergamos who suffered martyrdom for his failure to practice emperor worship.

APOCALYPSIS – Greek name for the book of Revelation, literally means "separating of the veil."

APOLLYON – (Rev. 9:11) Greek for "destroyer." *See* **Abaddon.**

APOSTASY/DISSENSION – (Rev. 2:2-5; 2:14-16,20-22; 3:1-2,14-19) (Isaiah 5:13; 24:5; 29:10,13; 60:2; Amos 8:11-12; Acts 20:29-30; 2 Thess. 2:1-4,11-12; 1 Tim. 4:1-2; 2 Tim. 3:1-7; 4:2-4; 1 John 4:1; 2 Peter 2:1-3,10; 3:3,16-17; 2 Nephi 32:7; D&C 86:2-3; 112:23) From Greek for "standing separately," its modern translation is "rebellion." Apostasy is characterized by division, spirit of rebellion against the Spirit of the Lord, corruption and lack of unity within a community, an organization, or group and may be religious, political or cultural in nature. Satan seeks to introduce apostasy into the Lord's

Church by means of corrupting individuals and the organization itself which in turn causes internal strife, contention, disagreements, hurt, and division. And then ignorance, darkness, false practices and idolatry prevail within the Latter-day Church, as alluded to in Rev. 13:7: "It was given unto him [Satan] to make war with the saints, and to overcome them" (Jeremiah 6:13-14; D&C 112:23). Apostasy in the last days, not unlike apostasy of the primitive Church, will take the following forms: 1.) The teaching of false doctrines and non-doctrine, persistent adherence to traditions and performances which by themselves have no redemptive power or significance, reliance upon "the arm of flesh," and materialism characterized by the admiration of wealth, success, power and influence; 2.) A willingness to compromise one's standards. In the last days a man will be expected to give and receive approval and approbation based on worldly standards and not God's; 3.) A weakening of resolve due to persecution and harassment from forces outside of the Lord's Church; 4.) The acceptance of uninspired or unauthorized teachers and leaders; 5.) Complacency and apathy; and, 6.) A loss of love and charitable behavior. In both modern and ancient times apostasy's most ugly trademark has been its persecution, neglect and indifference to the poor, weak, sick, disabled, orphans, widows, and strangers ['outsiders,' foreigners]. *See* Matthew, Chapters 23-25.

APOSTLES, TWELVE – (Rev. 18:20; 21:14) *See* **Twelve Apostles.**

ARK OF HIS TESTAMENT – (Rev. 11:19) Also known as the Ark of the Testimony or Ark of the Covenant.

ARMAGEDDON – (Rev. 16:16) (Joel 3:14; Zech. 14:1-2; Zeph. 3:7-8) The location where the last great battles take place that result in the ultimate destruction of the wicked and the ushering in of the millennium.

ARMIES IN HEAVEN – (Rev. 19:14) (D&C 88:112-115) The hosts of heaven that will follow Christ when He appears in glory at His Second Coming. These armies may consist of angels, resurrected and glorified beings, and possibly righteous mortals on earth that are caught up to be received by Christ at His coming. The key identifying feature of these hosts of heaven is that they are mounted upon "white horses" and "clothed in fine linen, white and clean."

ARRAYED – (Rev. 17:4; 19:8) Clothed in, adorned with.

AS IT WERE – (Rev. 4:1) A rhetorical phrase used a dozen times in the book of Revelation to describe the heavenly or supernatural in terms of what is more familiar, tangible and real.

ATONEMENT OF JESUS CHRIST – (Rev. 13:8; 19:13,15; 1:5-8) (1 Peter 1:18-20; Ether 3:14; 3 Nephi 11:10-14) The Messiah was foreordained and performed the assigned mission and the will of the Father in bringing about the Atonement (Genesis 49:11; Isaiah 63:2,5; D&C 133:48). In order to enjoy the benefits of the Atonement we are required to look to and focus on Christ and His sacrifice, grace and mercy. He was scourged and lifted up upon the cross (John 3:16-17) [Numbers 21:7-9: Not unlike Moses' instructions to the Israelites to look upon the brazen serpent fastened to a stick in order to be healed of deadly snake bites—Helaman 8:13-16] in order for us to experience healing, endurance, forgiveness of sin and receive eventual redemption and exaltation. We are then "washed of our sins in His blood" (Rev. 1:6; 7:14) (1 John 1:7) which is a figurative form of speech and is symbolized in mortality now by washing with water before entering a holy place such as the temple or even the presence of the Lord (Exodus 29:4; Hebrews 9:9-10), and by baptism and confirmation to receive the Gift of the Holy Ghost before becoming a member of His Latter-day Church. To believers the Atonement allows man to become part of the Lord's fold, dwell in peace and be fed by the Lamb, and be led to "living fountains of water: and God shall wipe away all tears from [our] eyes" (Rev. 7:17). This pastoral scene of calm and comfort represents a new spiritual and physical state of existence, which invokes images of the Millennium.

AUTHORITY – *See* **Priesthood.**

AVENGE – (Rev. 6:10) (Isaiah 1:24; 35:4; Heb. 10:30; Mormon 8:41) To execute judgment or punishment in behalf of the wronged or injured party against the offending party.

-*B*-

BABYLON – *See* **Materialism**; Name of the city whose people dominated the known world at the time of the fall of Judah. Its very name has come to symbolize all that is materialistic, worldly, evil, and wicked; The great and abominable church founded by the devil; During John's ministry, Rome symbolized Babylon. Nevertheless, throughout time, Babylon has become a code name applied to any power, empire or "great city, which reigneth over the kings of the earth" (Rev. 17:18). It is important to note that Babylon is not synonymous with "the beast." Babylon represents false worship, spurious ideologies, corrupt religion and immoral lifestyles. The heads and horns of the beast are symbolic of the worldly governments, kingdoms, powers, peoples and rulers in the world that have embraced the materialism and Babylonian way of life. Babylon exists independent of the beast and Babylon appears and grows in strength and power after the appearance of the beast. "In effect, after centuries of assimilation among the nations of the world, almost all of God's people have fallen into a deep sleep. They are weary and forgetful about keeping God's covenant while under Babylon's magic spell" (Avahram Giliadi, *Isaiah Decoded,* p. 120). The kingdoms and nations of the earth grew/grow in power and dominion as well. Babylon is synonymous with the term "great and abominable church," which is an immense, universal association of people or organizations bound together by their loyalty to that which God hates and principles that run contrary to the teachings of Christ. This "church" is involved specifically in oppressive efforts against the people of the world, illicit conduct, deception, immorality and idolatry. While the book of Revelation does not use the exact phrase "great and abominable church," both John and Nephi use a number of similar phrases to describe it (1 Nephi 13:4-9). They call it the "Mother of Harlots, and Abominations," "mother of abominations," and "the whore that sits upon many waters," (Rev. 17:1,5,12; 1 Nephi 14:10–11), and "the name[s] of blasphemy" (Rev. 13:1; 17:3). The term "Babylon" may also be a designation used to represent worldliness, materialism and wickedness in general. Characteristics of Babylon identified in both 1 Nephi and the book of Revelation include the following:

Babylon sheds the blood of the saints and the prophets (Rev. 16:6; 17:6; 18:24).

She is known for her enjoyment of extreme wealth and extravagant luxury (Rev. 17:4; 18:3,11-16).

She is characterized by sexual immorality and indulgent appetites (See Rev. 17:1-2, 5).

She has dominion over all nations (Rev. 17:15,18; 18:3, 23-24).

Her fate is to be destroyed and consumed by the very kings who, because of her deceptions, have made war on the Lamb, and the saints (Rev. 17:14-16; 18:23).

Jerusalem in her state of apostasy and corruption might serve as a type of Babylon, however, it is notable that the power of the "great and abominable church" and the modern Babylons were to arise "after the Apostles slept" (D&C 86:1–3) and originate within the Gentile kingdoms (1 Nephi 13:24–26).

In noting the characteristics of Babylon, it is important to distinguish between Babylon and the "beast" and the Anti-Christ. They do not represent necessarily the same things, though the beast and anti-Christ[s] support and uphold the great and abominable church (Rev. 17:3,7). Babylon, the "woman . . . arrayed in purple and scarlet" described in Revelation 17-18, is specifically the Satanic counterpart of the virtuous woman in chapter 12 who symbolizes the Church of Jesus Christ that was forced into the wilderness (Rev. 12:6)—that is, she became inaccessible to human beings.

[John's Revelation achieves its desired effect by contrasting conflicting images. Babylon stands in stark contrast to the woman Zion. For a brilliant summation of their conflicting qualities and opposites please refer to Avraham Gileadi's, *Isaiah Decoded*, pp.81-82.]

BABYLON, COME OUT OF – (Rev. 18:1-5) (Isaiah 48:20; 52:11; Jeremiah 51:6,9; Zech. 2:7; D&C 64:24; 133:5,7,14) The Lord has commanded that the Saints flee from Babylon. In some cases this could mean a physical move, but in most cases it is an injunction to join the cause of Zion and not be "partakers of her [Babylon's] sins."

BABYLON, FALL Of – (Rev. 14:8; 16:19; 17:16; 18: 2, 21) (Isaiah 21:9; Jeremiah 25:10; 51:8,34-46; D&C 1:15-16; 64:24; 88:105) When the sixth angel sounds his trump, it is to announce the destruction of Babylon, which will be done quickly and completely. The fall of Babylon includes the collapse of all political, economic and social institutions that profited from Babylon's reign of power.

BALAAM, DOCTRINE Of – (Rev. 2:14) (Num. 31:16; Deut. 23:4; 2 Peter 2:15; Jude 1:11) Form of false worship fashioned after the Old Testament prophet Balaam who tried to pervert the true worship of ancient Israel. This false worship was the practice of prophesying for money and gain and encouraged fornication and idolatry. The saints at Pergamos were rebuked by John for adhering to this apostate doctrine.

BALANCES, PAIR OF – (Rev. 6:5-6) Instrument used for weighing. It is carried by the third horseman of the Apocalypse and is a figurative representation of man's trials and tribulations. It ensures that equity will prevail in all the dealings between God and man.

BALAK/BALAC – (Rev. 2:14) King of the Moabites during the time of the false prophet Balaam and the exodus of the Israelites from Egypt. Since the Moabites could not defeat the Israelites in open battle, Balaam encouraged Balak to pervert the Israelites by encouraging fornication and idolatry among them.

BEAR – (Rev. 13:2) Satanic beast which arises from the sea and has feet "as the feet of a bear;" The ancient gray bear of Palestine, which grew up to six feet tall, inhabited the rocky and forested areas of Lebanon and Syria and was generally a solitary and shy creature feeding on berries and nuts. However, when hungry, threatened or angry, these bears became destructive and dangerous, and were opportunistic carnivores that quickly developed a taste for sheep. The beast is portrayed as having the feet of a bear possibly because it is with its massive paws and long claws that a bear inflicts the most damage. The bear has been traditionally associated with the empires of the Syrians, Medes and kingdoms to the north, and is mentioned as one of the mighty predator beasts of the earth that will coexist in peace with all of God's creatures during the Millennium (Proverbs 28:15; Isaiah 11:7; Dan. 7:5; Hosea 13:8; Amos 5:19).

BEAST – An image or symbol with alternating references to good and evil and to clean and unclean. One beast symbolizes the devil's kingdom where the seven heads and ten horns represent servants/leaders and the power of evil earthly kingdoms [the first beast which arose from the "sea" (Rev. 13:1-2) (Daniel 7:3-6,16-17)]. The corresponding righteous beast represents Christ's Church. The two main contrasted beasts that symbolize evil and good are the "Dragon" and the "Lamb" (Rev. 5:6). A second beast (Rev. 13:11) appears which is described as a deformed lamb and is interpreted as being a person such as a false prophet, anti-Christ, etc.; Person, power, or influence that upholds evil; (Rev. 4:6) (D&C 77:2-3) The four living creatures that surround God's throne are mentioned as being beasts. *See* **Four Beasts.** Note: Any confusion here is with the translation from the original Greek where several different words referring to different kinds of animals or creatures were all translated as "beast" in the King James Bible.

BEAST THAT . . . WAS, AND IS NOT, AND YET IS – (Rev. 17:8,11) Evil in some form or another is always allowed to exist on earth. When one face of evil is rejected or vanquished, another face arises to take its place in order to try and torment man until such time the returning Lord and the Archangel Michael lay hold upon the devil and cast him into perdition.

BEATITUDES – *See* **Blessings.** The Lord pronounces several blessings upon the righteous who listen to and heed the revelation given through His servant John. These blessings are generally referred to as *Beatitudes*.

BED, CAST INTO – (Rev. 2:22) (Job 33:19; Psalms 41:3) Bed of affliction, sickbed.

BEHOLD – (Rev. 1:18) This exclamation and imperative means "take heed," "pay attention," "listen and obey." [This term is found at least 24 times in the book of Revelation.]

BELOVED CITY— (Rev. 20:9) Jerusalem.

BERYL – Light green precious gem related to the emerald and aquamarine; Used in the foundation of the wall of the New Jerusalem (Rev. 21:20); Found in the breastplate of the High Priest (Ex. 28:20; 39:13); The color of the wheels in Ezekiel's vision was of that of beryl (Ezek. 1:16; 10:9). Has been variously translated as topaz, chrysolite.

BEWAIL – (Rev. 18:9) Lament, mourn over, feel sad for.

BIRD, UNCLEAN AND HATEFUL – (Rev. 18:2) (Ezek. 39:4) Scavengers, birds of prey that eat carrion; Evil spirits that torment man.

BIRTH, TRAVAILING IN – (Rev. 12:2) (1 Thess. 5:3) Expression of extreme distress and crisis, for example, the death of Christ and the relentless persecution of the early Christian Church; (Isaiah 66:7-9, Jeremiah 4:31; Micah 4:10) After any period of suffering, trial and disappointment, deliverance comes.

BLACK – (Rev. 6:5) (Job 30:30; Jeremiah 8:21; 14:2; Lament. 4:8; 5:10; Zech. 6:2,6) Color of the third horse of the Apocalypse. Black is a color representative of famine, plague, death, and mourning for someone deceased or something lost; May be indicative of a feeling of impending disaster or judgment; Absence of light; Evil desires of the heart; Treason; Abode of the dead.

BLASPHEME/SPEAK BLASPHEMIES – (Rev. 2:9; 13:5-6; 16:9,11,21) Revile or profane God or God's name; Falsely claim to be God or pretend to possess divine attributes and powers.

BLASPHEMY – (Rev. 13:1; 17:3) The name of the beast that arises from the sea. This name fits because it is the aim of the beast to supplant the one and only true God.

BLESSINGS FOR THE RIGHTEOUS and for those who hear or read this prophecy – (Rev. 1:3; 2:7,11,17,26; 3:4-5,12,21; 14:13; 16:15; 19:9; 20:6; 22:7,14) These blessings constitute **beatitudes** and each of them follow a consistent formula which urges the reader/listener to read/hear, understand, and do that which is pronounced in this book of prophecy. **Beatitudes** in this form appear at least seven times in the book of Revelation in the letter to the seven churches (and as expected, each of the **beatitudes** begins with the phrase "Blessed is . . ."); The covenant blessings foreseen by John the Seer before, during, and after great tribulation include but are not limited to: peace of mind, healing of body, soul and emotions through the acceptance of the Atonement of Jesus Christ, bounty and plenty, shelter and cover from the storm, freedom from fear, ability to exercise the priesthood, knowledge of God and Christ, and physical and spiritual deliverance from Babylon. The covenant blessings are predicated upon obedience, repentance, performance of required ordinances, gaining knowledge and understanding, and by receiving the Gift of the Holy Ghost; Those who read, study, understand and "**overcometh**" may expect the following blessings that John mentions:

They will partake of the "tree of life . . . in the paradise of God and inherit eternal life" (Rev. 2:7; 22:2,14).

"Blessed are the dead which die in the Lord," for they shall "rest from their labors; and their works do follow them" (Rev. 14:13).

They will not suffer the "second [or spiritual] death." They will become "priests of God and of Christ and shall reign with him a thousand years" (Rev. 2:11; 20:6; 20:14; 21:8) (Psalms 116:15).

They will be given "hidden manna" [the Bread of Life (John 6:51)], or in other words, a sure knowledge of Christ who is "hidden" to the non-believers and will receive a new name and a white stone. [From ancient and modern scripture we know that receiving a "new name" is proof or evidence of having entered into a covenant relationship and the "white stone" is a reference to God's acceptance and approval. It may also be a reference to the Urim and Thummim given to all those who enter into the celestial kingdom (D&C 130:10-11)] (Rev. 2:17).

They will receive the "**morning star**" (Rev. 2:28).

They will share with God power "over many kingdoms" and rule in glory as "kings and priests" (Rev. 1:5-6; 2:26; 5:9-10, 22:3).

Their name will not be removed from the Book of Life, and Christ will "confess their names" before the Father and the angels of Heaven and will clothe them in "white raiment" or in other words, celestial glory. While adorned in their "linen, clean and white," they will be invited to "walk with Christ" and be welcomed to the "marriage supper of the lamb" (Rev. 2:17; 3:2,5; 6:11; 7:14; 19:8-9,14; 21:27) (Matt. 10:32-33; 2 Tim. 2:12).

They will enter the temple [heaven] never to leave it again. They will receive the name of the Father and the Son, receive eternal life and become like God (D&C 93:20, 132:20); They will live in the New Jerusalem (Rev. 3:12).

They will share royal thrones with Heavenly Father and Jesus Christ and sit in their midst (Rev. 3:21; 4:2; 6:16) (Romans 8:17-18; Moses 7:59; D&C 84:33-38).

They will "keep [their] garments," or their sacred covenants in other words, and will not be ashamed if they remain watchful (Rev. 16:15).

They will inherit all that God has, and they will become the sons and daughters of Christ and He will accept them as His "called, and chosen, and faithful" (Rev. 17:14; 21:7) (Acts 17:29; Rom. 8:16-17; Gal. 4:7; Heb. 12:9; D&C 84:33-39).

See **Overcometh**.

BLIND – (Rev. 3:17) (2 Nephi 9:32) Refusing to accept or recognize the truth; Oblivious to or ignorant of the gravity of one's situation or condition.

BLOOD COME OUT OF THE WINEPRESS – (Rev. 14:20) Because the righteous blood of Jesus Christ was shed without the walls of the city, the wrath of God will come upon the wicked who have not been gathered together during the first harvest of the righteous. The destruction of the wicked, by war and other violent means, is likened to the treading of grapes in the winepress and their blood is compared to the wine coming from the clusters of fruit in the winepress.

BLOOD POURED OUT OF [the] VIAL – (Rev. 16:3-4) The pouring of blood from the vials upon the world represents curses executed upon the nations and peoples of the earth that could be understood at two different levels. The first explanation is that they represent the upheavals in nature and bloody conflicts that will engulf the world. The implication is that for the crime of shedding the blood of the prophets (Rev. 13:15; 16:6; 17:6; 18:24; 19:2) the evil peoples that remain on the earth will shed and consume, as it were, each other's blood (Isaiah 49:26). The second interpretation of this angelic act is that blood and destruction are indicative of the irreversible spiritual death of the wicked peoples of the world.

BLOOD, VESTURE DIPPED IN – (Rev. 19:13) (Isaiah 63:1-3; D&C 133:46-51) When Jesus comes a second time in glory, he will be clothed in red apparel, as though it had been "dipped in blood."

21

See **Red.** The blood red color of Christ's raiment is symbolic of the following: 1.) The shedding of His blood during the atoning sacrifice which took place in the Garden of Gethsemane and on the cross at Golgotha; 2.) The blood and sin of all those in this fallen world, especially those who have repented and accepted Christ as their Savior and Redeemer; and, 3.) The literal blood of the wicked unrepentant sinners who will be destroyed at the glory of His coming.

BLOOD, WATERS TO BE TURNED TO – (Rev. 8:8) (Psalms 78:44) *See* **Waters to be Cursed.**

BOOK/SCROLL – Record of events, thoughts, ideas, deeds and words that span given periods of time.

BOOK, ADD TO OR TAKE AWAY FROM THIS – (Rev. 1:3; 22:18–19) (Deut. 4:2; 12:32) Warning from John that no one is to tamper with the book of Revelation; More books were to come forward in the last days, that is, "revelations of God which shall come hereafter by the gift and power of the Holy Ghost, the voice of God, or the ministering of angels" (D&C 20:35).

BOOK OF LIFE – (Rev. 3:5; 20:12-13,15) (Dan. 12:1; Philip; 4:3. D&C 132:19) A record of the events of this world including the specific details of our lives. Our final judgment will be determined by what is recorded in this book. Elder Bruce R. McConkie writes that a record of our life is "transcribed in our souls" and that a record is "kept in heaven of the names and righteous deeds of the faithful" (DNTC, 3:578).

BOOK OF LIFE OF THE LAMB – (Rev. 13:8; 17:8; 21:27; 22:19) (Alma 5:57-58) Same as the Book of

Life.

BOOK[S] OF LIVES, WORKS, MISSION – (Rev. 20:12-13) (D&C 128:6-9) Deeds completed in mortality including ordinances of the priesthood.

BOOK SEALED WITH SEVEN SEALS – (Rev. 5:1-9) A book/scroll that contains the history of the world and (D&C 77:6-7) record of God's mysteries, will, designs and intents for this world and its people; Since the sealed scroll can only be opened by a specially qualified person, the sealed book must be some sort of legal document such as a will, testament, deed, contract or title and the opener who gives the reading of the scroll is the executor of the document who has satisfied or fulfilled the terms and conditions of the document.

BOOK, LITTLE – (Rev. 10:1-11) (D&C 77:14) Representation of John's ministry in which John was presented a little book by an angel and John swallowed it; (Jeremiah 15:16; Ezek. 2:9-10; 3:1-3) Jeremiah and Ezekiel had similar experiences.

BOOK, THE – (Rev. 5:1-5) (D&C 77:6–7) Story of the history of the world [kept and stored in heaven] that contains a summary of all happenings and works of individuals, societies, nations, etc. It includes documentation of all works, especially of the priesthood ordinances which are performed, and the mysteries, intentions and purposes of God concerning the world's temporal existence, as well; Story of one's personal mortal life, mission, destiny (Ex. 32:32-33; Luke 10:20); The heavenly book is most often described as being in the form of a scroll; Prophetic writing such as the book of Revelation (Rev. 1:11).

BOTTOMLESS PIT – *See* **Pit, Bottomless.**

BOW – (Rev. 6:2) The rider of the white horse of the Apocalypse holds a bow that is symbolic of the rider's warrior status and conquering ability.

BRASS – (Rev. 1:15; 2:18) "Feet like unto fine brass" symbolizes that the Lord stands as the righteous and perfect judge of mankind, with brass representing refinement [purity], stability, strength and permanence. The words "brass" and "bronze" have not been translated consistently in various editions of the Bible and are used interchangeably (Job 40:18; Ezek. 1:7; Dan. 7:19; 10:6).

BREADTH OF THE EARTH – (Rev. 20:9) Wide expanse, greater part of the earth.

BREASTPLATES [of Iron/Fire] – (Rev. 9:9,17) Swarms of "locusts" possibly represent the massive movements of armored troops who wear bullet-proof vests and helmets, and are protected in their vehicles of reinforced steel.

BRIDE/BRIDEGROOM – (Rev. 18:23; 21:2,9; 22:17) The Lord's relationship with believers is often described in the context of a marriage with the Lord being the Bridegroom and the Church or the New Jerusalem/Israel being the Bride (Isaiah 49:18; 54:5; 61:10; 62:5; Jeremiah 2:2; 5:7; Ezek. 16:28; Hos. 2:19; John 3:29; Gal. 4:26; 2 Cor. 11:2; Eph. 5:26-27; D&C 33:17; 88:92; 109:74; 133:10,19).

BRIDLES, HORSE — *See* Horse Bridles.

BRIGHT AND MORNING STAR – Jesus Christ (Rev. 22:16).

BRIMSTONE – (Rev. 9:17; 14:10; 19:20; 20:10; 21:8) (Gen. 19:24-25; Deut. 29:23; Job 18:15; Psalms

11:6; Isaiah 30:33; 34:8-10; Ezek. 38:22; Luke 17:29) Combustible sulfur compound that spontaneously bursts into flame; Symbolic of divinely inflicted torment and retribution. Used commonly in the phrase "fire and brimstone."

BRONZE – (Rev. 9:20) Alloy of tin and copper, often translated as "brass;" Common inexpensive metal used to make idols.

BROTHER – (Rev. 1:9) (Proverbs 18:9; Job 30:29) Form of address indicating fondness and closeness in terms of relationship, situation, experience, likeness or character. John begins his letter [The Revelation] to the churches identifying himself as their "brother, and companion in tribulation . . . ."

- $\mathscr{C}$ -

CAGE – (Rev. 18:2) Babylon, the false religious system, is likened to a cage where the hold and grip upon its occupants are so strong that it is impossible to escape. When Babylon falls, her mortal inhabitants will be destroyed, hence the only remaining citizens will be "devils," "every foul spirit" and "every unclean and hateful bird."

CAMP OF THE SAINTS — (Rev. 20:9) Places where the saints will be located and gathered in order to withstand the attacks of the adversary.

CANDLE/CANDLESTICK – (Rev. 1:12-13,20; 4:5; 11:4) (Matt. 5:15) The Church, bearer and custodian of light [truth], but not originator of light; Translated also as "lamp;" The two special witnesses/prophets spoken of in Chapter 11 of the Revelation are likened to "two candlesticks" (Rev. 11:4); (Proverbs 20:27) The spirit of man; (Psalms 119:105) Truth, the word of God "which is a lamp unto my feet, and a light unto my path."

CANDLE, LIGHT OF A – (Rev. 18:23; 22:5) The light of the candle, in any of its interpretations, will not exist in future Babylon because Babylon will receive the rewards of darkness and annihilation that she deserves. Nor will the man-made or natural sources of light be necessary in the New Jerusalem, because God and Christ will be the light there.

CANDLESTICKS, TWO – (Rev. 11:4) The two special witnesses spoken of in Chapter 11 of John's Revelation are likened to two candlesticks. *See* **Witnesses, Two.**

CARNELIAN – (Rev. 21:20) Brownish-red variety of chalcedony, also known as Sardine or Sardonyx; Included on the breastplate of the high priest; Precious stone found in the foundation of the wall of the New Jerusalem.

CARBUNCLE – (Isaiah 54:12) Variously translated as feldspar, emerald, beryl, garnet; Found on the high priest's breastplate (Exodus 28:17; 39:10); According to Isaiah it is to be used in making the gates of the New Jerusalem. (Rev. 21:21) John doesn't make mention of a stone by this name. The inconsistency between John's and Isaiah's description of the city's gates is not important in that both prophets saw that the gates were made of very beautiful material of inestimable value and gave an account of their individual perceptions as such.

CARRIED AWAY IN THE SPIRIT – *See* **Spirit, In The.**

CAST DUST/ASHES ON HEAD – (Rev. 18:19) Act of mourning and grief.

CAST OUT/DOWN – (Rev. 12:4,8-10,13) (Isaiah 14:12; D&C 29:36-39) Prior to our mortal existence there was a "war in heaven" between Satan and the Father (Rev. 12:7). The devil and his "angels," or "stars of heaven," were thrown out of their heavenly abode and now dwell amidst man on earth where they tempt and afflict mortals.

CENSER – (Rev. 8:3-5) (Num. 16:17; Heb. 9:4) Vessel used for the offering and burning of incense (Lev. 10:1). It is used in connection with worshipping at the altar of God; Container or bowl used for carrying live coals; (Psalms 141:1-2) Symbolic of prayer, intercession and worship.

CHAIN, GREAT – (Rev. 20:1) (Psalms 73:6; 149:8; Lament. 3:7; Ezek. 7:23; Acts 28:20; 2 Peter 2:4; Jude 1:6; Moses 7:26) Symbol of binding, judgment, burden or oppression.

CHALCEDONY – (Rev. 21:19) Alternate translation for agate. Includes in its definition carnelian, chrysoprasus, flint, jasper and onyx. Stone included in the foundation of the wall of the New Jerusalem.

CHARIOT – (Rev. 9:9) (Psalms 20:7; 76:6; 104:3; Isaiah 66:15; Jeremiah 4:13; Ezek. 39:20; Dan. 11:40; Joel 2:5; Zech. 6:1-3; Hab. 3:8) Vehicle symbolic of swiftness, power and strength in going into battle. The power and terror of the chariots and horses in battle is overwhelming, yet the power and might of God is greater.

CHASTEN – (Rev. 3:19) To admonish, instruct. "As many as I love, I rebuke and chasten: be zealous therefore, and repent" (Heb. 12:6, D&C 136:31, Mosiah 23:21); *See* **Affliction/Adversity.**

CHILDREN – (Rev. 2:23) (1 Peter 1:14) Followers, disciples, adherents; (1 Cor. 13:11; 14:20; Eph. 4:14) Type for those lacking maturity or who are under guardianship.

CHRYSOLITE – (Rev. 21:20) Yellow form of the mineral topaz and beryl (Ezekiel 1:16; 10:9; 28:13). Precious stone included in the foundation of the wall of the New Jerusalem.

CHRYSOPRASUS – (Rev. 21:20) Green variety of chalcedony; Precious stone found in the foundation of the wall of the New Jerusalem.

CITY OF GOD – (Rev. 3:12) (Heb. 11:16) *See* **New Jerusalem.**

CITY, THE GREAT/MIGHTY – (11:8) Jerusalem in its state of apostasy; Babylon (Rev. 14:8; 16:19; 17:18; 18:10,16,21).

CITY, THE HOLY/BELOVED – (Rev. 11:2; 20:9; 21:2) (Neh. 11:1; Isaiah 52:1) Jerusalem; The New Jerusalem; (Moses 7:19) City of Enoch which is to return to earth from heaven during the millennial reign (Rev. 21:2) (Moses 7:62–64; D&C 84:100).

CLEANSING OF THE CHURCH – (Rev. 14:18-19) (D&C 63:32-34; 97:25-28; 112:24-26; 133:2; Ezek. 9:6; 1 Peter 4:17-19; Matthew 23:26; Alma 60:23) In interpreting the parable of the 'wheat and the tares' the Prophet Joseph likened the wheat to faithful saints and the tares to the apostates, wrong-doers and sinners within the Latter-day Church. In all gospel dispensations the tares, a type of weed identical in appearance to wheat, have been allowed to grow beside the wheat and are not quickly uprooted and destroyed for fear of unintentional damage to the wheat. However, the Lord will not come to return and reign over a polluted and unclean people and the judgments of God will begin within the Church itself. The Lord has promised that "Zion shall escape if she observe to do all things whatsoever I have commanded her" (D&C 97:25). Elder Bruce R. McConkie wrote concerning the wrath of God: "There is a certain smugness in the Church, a feeling that all these things are for others . . . [but] . . . the saints in the Church and the Gentiles in the world will both be judged by the same standard – the standard of Christ" (*The Millennial Messiah*, p. 502). Elder McConkie taught further that "any congregation of saints which is not true and faithful shall lose its place in the true Church" (DNTC 3:446); President Joseph F. Smith (*Gospel Doctrine*, p. 312) and Ezra Taft Benson (CR, Apr.1986; Apr.1989) have stated that there is a great need to cleanse the inner vessel in regard to three serious matters: 1.) Obey the law of chastity; 2.) Reject soundly "false educational ideas" of the modern day secular institutions; and, 3.) Overcome pride by becoming meek and humble (Isaiah 13:11; D&C 112:10); President Benson warned that only repentance and "humility can turn away" God's approaching anger upon the Church (Mosiah 26:36; Alma 6:2-4; D&C 97:22-28). President Joseph F. Smith's remarks in conference confirm the preceding statements: "Unless the Latter-day Saints will live their religion, . . . they will be the first to fall beneath the judgments of the Almighty, for His judgments will begin at His own house" (CR, April 1880, p. 96).

CLEANSING OF THE EARTH – (Rev. 8:7-8; 16:8-9) (Isaiah 33:14-16; Joel 2:30; D&C 5:18-19; 97:22-24; 135:6) The earth must be cleansed of its impurities and sinful inhabitants before Christ comes to reign in glory, and this will primarily be done by means of fire; Throughout the scriptures fire is often associated with God's judgments and punishment of the wicked [note the destruction of Sodom and Gomorrah, Genesis 19:24-28] and fire conjures up very powerful and vivid images to the mind. [Compare 1 Kings 1:12 to Rev. 20:9.] In Luke 9:51-56 the Apostles wanted Jesus to call down fire from heaven to destroy those who rejected the Messiah; Fire [and smoke/cloud] is indicative of God's presence. (Rev. 15:1-8) (Isaiah 6:3-4); (Rev. 16:17-21) (D&C 87:6) Other means used to cleanse the earth will be earthquakes, lightning, thundering and a great hail storm. This punishing judgment spoken of in this part of Revelation will bring about the prophesied "full end of all nations." *See* **Curses.**

CLOUD/SMOKE/FIRE – (Rev. 10:1; 11:12; 14:14-16; 15:8) (Ex. 13:20; 19:18; Isaiah 6:4; 19:1; Ezek. 1:4; Matt. 17:5; Acts 1:9; D&C 34:7; 84:5) Glory, divine power; Cloud of smoke or fire often indicates the presence and guidance of God.

CLOUD[S] – (Rev. 1:7) (Psalms 104:3; Dan. 7:13-14; Matt. 24:30; Mark 13:26; 1 Thess. 4:17; Heb. 12:1; D&C 45:16,44; 76:63) In phrases such as: "return in clouds," "clouds of glory," "clouds of witnesses," the clouds represent those groups of people [prophetic servants, saints, angels, etc.] redeemed by Christ who will be with Him at His second coming (D&C 84:5). They will be heirs to His glory, thus giving rise to a conceptual connection between Christ's glory, the redeemed saints, and increased divine power and glory (2 Cor. 3:18). Angels which appear in glory, come as "with a cloud" or "on a cloud," indicating their exalted status (Rev.10:1).

CLUSTER OF THE VINE – (Rev. 14:18) (Isaiah 65:8; Micah 7:1) Symbolic of the gathering of selected groups; (Matt. 7:15-20) Representative of the fruit of the vine.

COMPASSED – (Rev. 20:9) Surrounded, encircled, encompassed.

CONFESS – (Rev 3:5) (Matt 10:32; D&C 45:3-5; Moses 7:39) Commend, praise, acknowledge.

CORRUPT – (Rev. 19:2) To defile, pollute, cause to decay or become rotten.

COUNTENANCE – (Rev. 1:16) Appearance, presence.

COURT, OUTER – (Rev. 11:2) (Psalms 135:2; Zech. 3:7) Environs of the temple reserved for the Gentiles and others excluded from entering the temple itself.

CROWN[S] – (Rev. 2:10; 3:11; 4:4, 10; 6:2; 9:7; 12:1,3; 13:1; 14:14) (1 Cor. 9:25; 2 Tim. 2:5; 4:8; 1 Peter 5:4; James 1:12; D&C 75:5; 78:15) As in 'Crown of life.' Eternal life and redemption from the afflictions of the world; Crown may be a symbol of power, authority, position of dominion [mortal or divine], royalty, priesthood or victory. The early Latter-day Saints were promised that if they built a temple unto the Lord and remained "faithful in all things" they would be blessed with a crown of "honor, immortality and eternal life" (D&C 124:55); The Dragon [Satan] and the Beast are only allotted a confined number of crowns while the crowns of the Son of God are limitless and without number (Rev. 19:12). The "crowns like gold" worn by the locusts that are to afflict the world is likely a descriptive statement in referring to metal helmets worn by modern troops in battle. *See* **Locusts.**

CRYSTAL – (Rev. 4:6; 21:11; 22:1) The **"sea of glass"** and the "river of **water of life**" are compared to crystal; Translated from original word for **quartz** and has been rendered variously as ice, **jasper**, **pearl**, and alabaster in Biblical manuscripts. **Crystal** as used in the context here in Revelation is a representation of the purity, clarity, and brilliance of the celestial kingdom. The **New Jerusalem** is described as having the appearance of being "clear as **crystal**," suggesting that it has a translucent or radiant quality.

CUBIT – (Rev. 21:17) Unit of measure equal to about 20 inches. The wall of the New Jerusalem is 144 cubits high. The number 144 is likely symbolic representing the number 12 multiplied by itself.

CUP – (Rev. 14:10; 16:19; 18:6) (Psalms 11:6; 23:5; 75:8; Isaiah 51:17-22; Jeremiah 49:12; Ezek. 23:33; Matt. 26:39,42; John 18:11; Mosiah 5:5; D&C 19:18; 29:17; 43:26; 101:11; 103:3) Metaphor for a vessel that contains the essence of any number of experiences or qualities. Used in expressions such as "cup of [his] indignation;" (3 Nephi 11:11) Fate, lot, destiny; (Rev. 17:4) (Jeremiah 51:7) The woman Babylon, in mocking imitation of the Lord and His angels, holds a golden cup but it is full of "abominations and filthiness of her fornication." At the time of judgment, her cup will be filled double with the wrath of God. *See* **Drunk.**

CURSES/PLAGUES/WOES – Considering that John recorded the Revelation as a message of hope and comfort in order to assure the saints that the cause of the Christ will triumph on earth, unenlightened modern-day readers seem to fret and obsess over the many catastrophes, disasters, plagues and destruction that are mentioned in the Apocalypse. It's logical to assume that if blessings await those saints who endure well with patience for the Lord and who keep their covenants, then misfortune and negative consequences are in store for: 1.) Those saints that break their covenants and fight against the Truth or turn their loyalties and labors to the cause of Babylon; 2.) Those who have had an adequate chance to accept the Christ and reject Him; and, 3.) Of course, those evil-doers whose works result in corruption, violence, suffering of others, and death, especially the death and martyrdom of the saints (Rev. 6:9-11; 9:20-21; 16:9-11); In the same way that John made record of the blessings for the righteous, he writes of the curses that await the apostates, persecutors of the saints, idolaters, and evil-doers:

The gospel, Holy Ghost, priesthood and God's callings and approval will be denied to the unworthy.

The wicked will not be satisfied with persecuting that which is good. They will turn upon each other causing universal exploitation, corruption and violence.

God will no longer allow man to prosper by "the arm of flesh" and the works of Babylon will perish. This will result not only in a total loss of peoples' labor and the property accumulated during their life's work, but also in the hardening of their hearts against God to the point that multitudes will blaspheme God and suffer the "second death" (Isaiah 28:15). This second death will separate them both physically and spiritually from their Father in Heaven forever.

Hearts will become hardened, the Light will be extinguished and minds will go dark. Satan will inspire man to contrive and do all manner of evil, meaning that as the world ripens for destruction love, charity, faith and service (Rev. 2:19) will be rare commodities and likely found only among the saints that successfully escaped from Babylon.

Fear, despair, anger, fatigue, bondage of all kinds [including financial], emotional and spiritual illnesses, deception, sorcery, etc., will torment mankind. [These types of torments, symbolized by the locusts and scorpions in John's text, may be what is alluded to in Revelation 9:1-10, that is, the "locusts" and "scorpions" will only have power to "hurt men," "that they should not kill them," but men will "desire to die, but death will flee from them."]

Disease, illnesses, and plagues will occur which to a large degree will be like the ones that afflicted Egypt prior to the great Exodus (Deut 28:60). This is noticeable as John describes the judgments of God that follow the sounding of the trumpets and the pouring of the wrath of God from the vials/bowels of the altar upon the earth. It is noteworthy that prior to the end of the world the plagues of ancient Egypt and other "major events of antiquity will have a second fulfillment–History is going to repeat itself in a big way" (Avraham Gileadi, *Isaiah Decoded*, p. 25).

Natural disasters such as earthquakes, floods, famine, hail, drought, violent storms, fire, etc., will be frequent, universal and catastrophic in nature.

War and large-scale violence perpetrated against entire nations will become the rule of the day, and, based on the principle of dualism [types and patterns] most modern scholars believe the future wars will be for the senseless and self-serving purposes of building and destroying entire empires and nations according to man's selfishness, lust, and greed, much like the cruelty and wars after the manner set into motion by the ancient Assyrians, Babylonians, and Romans.

Note that the righteous saints will be alive to witness these disasters and will survive (D&C 87:6,8; 97:24-25). Some of them will perish but will receive eternal life and the glory of God. John also makes specific mention that these horrific judgments will come as a result of the prayers and petitions of the true saints/martyrs who have longed for justice and vengeance upon those who have sought to "destroy the earth" (Rev. 11:18; 16:1,5-7). In reality, this 'laundry list' of woes and plagues should logically fall under the category of blessings for the saints since the true saints will not fear the curses and plagues (Isaiah 26:3-4). The faithful saints will be protected by the power of the priesthood. They will see and recognize the hand of God in the earthquakes, thunder and lightning and there will be peace and comfort in the midst of violent shaking and perplexities for "in the latter days [they] shall consider it perfectly" (Jeremiah 23:20).

CURSE, NO MORE – (Rev. 22:3) The earth will be restored to its same primal and pristine condition as at the time of creation. The earth will appear as the Garden of Eden and spiritual death will be eliminated since God and His Son will dwell in the midst of the **New Jerusalem**.

DAINTY THINGS – (Rev. 18:7,14) Pleasures of sin; The devil's pampering delicacies and delightful desires; Excessive wealth and extravagance (Proverbs 23:3).

DARKNESS – (Rev. 16:10) (Isaiah 50:3; 59:2; Amos 8:9; 1 John 1:5-6; D&C 82:5; 112:23) Ignorance, absence of light or truth; (Isaiah 60:2; Moses 7:61) Apostasy; (Amos 5:18-20; Joel 2:2; Zeph 1:15) Final punishment of the wicked, for whom the final judgment and the coming of the Lord in glory will be a day of darkness. (Deut. 28:28-29; Exodus 10:21-23) The "**smoke of the pit**" may be the source of darkness and represents the torments and temptations that the devil inflicts upon mankind (Rev. 9:2) (Isaiah 8:21-22; 1 Nephi 12:17; D&C 84:49); Captivity; Blackness (Isaiah 42:7; 47:5).

DAVID – (Rev. 5:5; 22:16) *See* **Root of David.**

DAY OF THE LORD – *See* **Lord's Day.**

DEAD – (Rev. 3:1) (Eph. 2:1) Because of their sins and transgressions the saints in Sardis became dead as pertaining to things of the spirit.

DEADLY WOUND – (Rev. 13:3,12) The beast that emerged from the sea had seven heads, one of which was "wounded to death." If the heads of the beast represent the prominent rulers of the nations, then the wounded head pertains to a ruler that appeared to have perished but somehow revives and regains power. If the heads represent dominant worldly philosophies and heresies, then the wounded head represents a doctrine that seemingly went out of style or was rejected but later arises to universal popularity. The important point is that the healing of the wound appears so dramatic and unexpected that people will be in awe and amazement. This healing stands mockingly in contrast to the crucified Lord and Him raised by God from the dead.

DEATH – (Rev. 6:8) The name of the fourth Horseman of the Apocalypse. One named "Hell" accompanies "Death" to receive the bodies of the slain who die by the sword, famine, plague and wild beasts — the "four sore judgments" according to Ezekiel (Ezek. 14:21). At the final judgment "Death" and "Hell" are required to deliver up their dead for Christ holds the "keys of hell and of death" (Rev. 1:18). And they whose names are "not found written in the book of life" will subsequently be "cast into the lake of fire" with the beast, the false prophet and the devil. (Rev. 20:14-15) *See* **Second Death.** The Lord assures us that "he will wipe away every tear

from [our] eyes, and death shall be no more" (Rev.
21:4) (1 Cor. 15:54; 2 Nephi 9:26; Alma 11:45).

DELIVERANCE – (Rev. 7:9-17) (Joel 2:32; 3 Nephi
10:12; D&C 45:35; 97:25) *See* **Salvation**. The wrath
of God will be poured out upon the earth with such
fierceness that all will echo John's question, "Who
shall be able to stand?" (Rev. 6:17) (Psalms 76:7)
We are promised that even as the wicked will be
consumed "by fire," the righteous will be preserved.
"Wherefore, the righteous need not fear; for thus
saith the prophet, they shall be saved, even if it so be
by fire" (1 Nephi 22:17). Once one has accepted
Christ, entered into the covenant and has had his
sins washed away by "the blood of the Lamb,"
Christ's atoning sacrifice becomes effective in one's
life and "mercy can satisfy the demands of justice,
and encircles them in the arms of safety" (Alma
34:16). The Prophet Isaiah records it this way [in
modern English]: "Fear not: for I call you by name;
you are mine . . . when you walked through the fire
. . . I was your Savior . . . you are precious in my
sight; you are honorable and I love you" (*See* Isaiah
43:1-4). In the same way that abiding by the terms
of the Atonement delivers one from sin, deliverance
also alludes to the act of a physical rescue from the
forces of evil in the **last days** (Rev. 19:11-16) (2
Kings 6:13–18). Even though "peace shall be taken
from the earth, and the devil shall have power over
his own dominion" we can take comfort in the fact
that "the Lord shall have power over his saints, and
shall reign in their midst" (D&C 1:35-36).

DESOLATE – (Rev. 17:16; 18:19) Abandoned,
forsaken; Barren, lifeless.

DEVIL – *See* entries for **Accuser** and **Satan.** (Rev. 12:10,12; 20:2) **Devil** comes from the Greek for *slanderer, faultfinder, accuser.* "Woe to the inhabiters of the earth . . . for the devil is come down unto you, having great wrath, because he knows that he hath but a short time." The devil desires to thwart God's purposes by seeking to deceive and destroy the souls of God's children and deprive them of their divine and intended birthright (Isaiah 14:12–16; 1 Peter 5:8; D&C 1:35; 10:27).

DISSENSION – *See* **Apostasy.**

DIVINE – Godly; One who foresees and prophesies.

DOG – (Rev. 22:15) An "unclean" animal because, like a jackal, it is a scavenger; Term of derision for Gentiles used by the Jews; (Isaiah 56:10-11; Philip 3:2; 2 Peter 2:21-22) Wicked person, evil or false leader or teacher, hypocrite.

DOMINION – (Rev. 1:6) Power, might, dominance.

DOOR – (Rev. 3:8,20) Barrier that is literal/physical or metaphorical. The "open door" that "no man can shut" is likely the gate to heaven (2 Nephi 9:41); The door at which Jesus stands and knocks is the way to our heart or mind (Isaiah 55:6-7; D&C 88:63); For John to receive and understand the vision, a door to heaven had to open (Rev. 4:1); Opportunity (Acts 14:27; 1 Cor. 16:9; Col. 4:3).

DOUBLE UNTO HER, DOUBLE ACCORDING TO HER WORKS – (Rev. 18:6) (Isaiah 40:2; Jeremiah 16:18) Under the law of Moses transgressors were to be punished two-fold for their crimes. For example, a thief was to repay **double** what had been stolen. **Babylon** is to be punished two-fold for her crimes and sins against the Lord and His people.

DRAGON, RED – **Devil**, **Satan**, old serpent, **serpent**, Lucifer, adversary (Rev. 12:3-4,7,9,13,16-17; 13:2,4,11; 16:13; 20:2) (Isaiah 27:1; 51:9; Dan. 7:7-8).

DRINK – (Rev. 14:8,10; 16:6) (Isaiah 28:7-8) *See* **Drunk.**

DRUNK – (Rev. 17:2,6; 18:3) (Isaiah 29:9-10; Jeremiah 25:27; 51:7; 1 Nephi 22:13-14) Reveling in sin and evil including uncontrolled indulgence into the lusts of the flesh and murder of righteous saints; Saturated, fullness of indulgence; Spiritually insensitive, apostate; Consumed and intoxicated with the wickedness of **Babylon**. *See* **Wine.**

DUST, CAST — (Rev. 18:19) (Acts 22:23) *See* **Cast dust.**

-ℰ-

EAGLE – Term translated alternately as *angel* (Rev. 8:13).

EAGLE, GREAT – (Rev. 4:7; 12:14) The imagery of an **eagle** with **great wings**, all throughout the prophetic writings, has represented God's power of deliverance (Ex. 19:4; Deut. 32:11; Psalms 103:5; Isaiah 40:31); In tradition the **eagle** is known for being both the most caring and nurturing of all birds and is also the most majestic and swiftest of God's creatures. It is often associated with deity, royalty and priesthood [Egyptian and Babylonian tradition]; The **eagle** was the emblem of the tribe of Dan which was the tribe of Israel situated farthest to the north geographically; In John's vision the fourth beast which guards the throne of God is like unto a **great flying eagle.**

EARTH – Sometimes used as a metaphor for worldliness or materialism though this image is not justified since comparing the words **earthy** and **worldly** becomes conceptually and semantically problematic because of the diverse and individualized usage and interpretations of the terms. In the writings of John, **earth** is *not* a synonym for the term **world** (Rev. 10:2,5). **Earth** is the dry, land portion of this mortal world/planet upon which man dwells, and does not include within its definition the sea, the skies or parts beneath the earth. Mortal man's body is made of the elements of the earth.

EARTH AND HEAVEN FLED AWAY – (Rev. 20:11) *See* **New Earth/New Heaven.**

EARTH IS SHAKEN/EARTHQUAKE – (Rev. 6:12-13; 8:5; 11:13,19; 16:18) (Isaiah 13:13; 29:6; Ezek. 38:19-20; Joel 2:30-31; 3:16; Hag. 2:6-7; Heb. 12:26-28; D&C 45:33; 49:23; 84:117-118; 87:6; 88:87; 133:31; Moses 7:61) Earthquakes and the literal and figurative shaking of the earth and nations upon the earth are signs of the last days and signal the closing of the sixth seal and opening of the seventh seal in the history of the earth. Some of the earthquakes mentioned in Revelation are associated with the judgments of God upon the world, others pertain to the final destruction of the world and restoration to its original form and appearance as at the beginning.

EAST – (Rev. 7:2) (D&C 77:9) The sun rises in the East; (Matt. 24:27) Jesus Christ will come again or appear in glory from the **East**. Biblical tradition points to the belief that both great blessings and God's judgments come from or have their origin in the East.

EAST, KINGS OF THE – (Rev. 16:12) Allusion to the ancient rulers who advanced and warred against kingdoms and nations to their west. This reference serves as a shadow of the gathering of the mighty kingdoms that will come together for the final battles against Israel in the last days.

EAT HER [BABYLON'S] FLESH – (Rev. 17:16) (Isaiah 9:19-20; 49:26) Jesus brought forth a doctrine that provides for the eventual physical and spiritual regeneration and renewal of man. Satan, through his church "Babylon," hocks an ideology and religion of decadence and destruction. The reader is invited to contrast the Christian saint's reverential partaking of the sacramental emblems in memory of Jesus with the feeding frenzy of the insatiable citizens of Babylon who indulge their appetites to the point that they destroy both themselves and Babylon.

EGYPT – Name of a country or countries which came to symbolize spiritual bondage. Egypt is equated with Sodom and both are used as metaphors or symbols for a wicked and apostate Jerusalem of the latter days (Rev. 11:8). It is worth noting that the plagues and curses that came upon ancient Egypt as recorded in Exodus are repeated in one form or another as coming at the time of the Lord's final judgments upon the world.

EIGHTH – (Rev. 17:11,13) There is an **eighth** "ruler" implicated with the "**seven** rulers" symbolized by the **seven** heads of the beast. The wicked intent of the "seven rulers" is derived from the devil, the evil mastermind and **eighth** ruler, who with the rulers "have one mind, and shall give their and power and strength unto the beast."

ELDERS, FOUR AND TWENTY – (Rev. 4:1-2,4,10; 5:8,14; 7:11; 11:16; 19:4) (D&C 77:5) According to modern revelation these 24 elders were identified as individual priesthood holders in the ancient church who remained true and faithful to their calling and thereafter received white robes, symbols of their sanctification, and gold crowns, symbolic of their celestial status and worthiness to sit in thrones alongside their Heavenly Father. The elders' names are not known, and it is not clear whether the number 24 is being used symbolically or literally.

EMERALD – (Rev. 4:3; 21:19) Bright green form of **beryl**; The **emerald** was found on the high priest's breastplate (Ex. 39:11) and included in the foundation of the wall of the **New Jerusalem**; John describes the **throne** of God being surrounded by an emerald color **rainbow**. The radiant green color of the **emerald** suggests life and eternity.

END OF THE WORLD – *See* **World, End of.**

ENDURE WELL TO THE END – (Rev. 2:2-3,19,25; 3:10-11; 13:10; 14:12) (Luke 21:19; James 5:7-11; 1 Nephi 13:37; 2 Nephi 31:20; D&C 14:7; 54:10; Isaiah 40:28-31) The message of John's Revelation is one of comfort, hope and courage. It is meant to give assurance that Good will ultimately and inevitably triumph over evil in spite of the terrible afflictions and adversity that are to beset mankind. Having patience as John describes and enduring to the end is a true form of worship (D&C 93:19-20) that will ultimately result in deliverance and is an indication of an individual's "divine nature" (2 Peter 1:4-10). The Apostle Paul's words are applicable here: "We are troubled on every side, yet not distressed; we are perplexed but not in despair; persecuted but not forsaken; cast down but not destroyed" (2 Cor. 4:8-9); The "patience of the saints" written of by John is expressed by Elder Neal Maxwell who reminds us of the challenges of experiencing the bitter in the world "without becoming bitter" (**CR**, Oct. 1997), to resist the urge to retaliate and revile those that revile the truth and that which is good (1 Peter 3:8-9); Enduring means to be refined by adversity, cleansed and made whole as it is written in Revelation 3:18: "I counsel thee to buy of me gold tried in the fire, that thou mayest be rich; and white raiment, that thou mayest be clothed, and that the shame of thy nakedness do not appear; and anoint thine eyes with eyesalve, that thou mayest see."

EPHESUS – (Rev. 1:11; 2:1-7) Prominent political and commercial center and river port of the Roman Empire in Asia during the ministries of the Lord's Apostles; John warns the saints of the importance of retaining their fervor and love for Chris. He also warns them of the evil of going through the motions of righteousness for the sake of appearance and tradition, yet losing their understanding of the compassion and charity which are what should truly motivate their service to others. John tells them to forsake and not condone false philosophies.

EUPHRATES RIVER – (Rev. 9:14; 16:12) Interpreted as being a boundary beyond which the destroying angels are not allowed to proceed until authorized to do so. The Euphrates River represented a natural boundary between Israel and the powers of Assyria and Babylon to the north. The dried Euphrates is symbolic of the removal of God's protection from wicked Israel.

EVEN SO, AMEN – (Rev. 1:7) Amen and Amen. "Even so" is the Greek rendition for the Hebrew word "Amen."

EVERLASTING GOSPEL – (Rev. 14:6) (D&C 88:103-104; 135:3) On a literal and specific level the "everlasting gospel" is the Book of Mormon which was delivered into the hands of the Prophet Joseph Smith by the angel Moroni.

EXALTATION/CELESTIAL STATE OF THE EARTH – (Rev. 21:1 through 22:5) (Isaiah 65:17; D&C 29:24-25; 93:1-9) *See* **New Heaven/New Earth.** All things will become new, as a new earth and a new heaven, brilliant as jewels and a sea of glass like crystal. The exalted habitations will be as refined as pure gold and built as if it were with precious gems, the earth itself will become God's celestial temple and throne. The intelligence, knowledge, glory and power of God, His Christ and their children will be such that there will be no night and no need for the sun, moon or stars or candles. Those who enter therein will be the kings and nations of the earth that bring glory and honor and will be deserving to see the face of their Savior whose name they took upon themselves in a pre-mortal life and again in this mortal life.

EYES – (Rev. 4:6-8) (D&C 77:4) Symbols for light, brilliance, character, knowledge and understanding; (Rev.5:6) Angels and servants of God; (Rev. 1:14; 2:18; 19:12) (Dan. 10:6) When used in prophetic speech as applied to the risen Lord and King, His **eyes** are described as being **flames of fire**, the **fire** as is a symbolic reference to divine presence. The Prophet Joseph, for lack of more eloquent words, could only describe the **eyes** of our glorified Master as "flames of fire" (D&C 110:3); (Rev. 1:7; 3:18; 19:12; 21:4) Sensory organ of the body through which we perceive information about the world around us in the form of images. It is also an organ which frequently reveals information about an individual's inner feelings and emotions, as well as spiritual and physical well-being.

EYE SALVE – (Rev. 3:18) The early saints of Laodicea were spiritually blind and did not see things in the same light that God does. Therefore, the Lord commands them to "anoint [their] eyes" in order to see that they are lagging and weak in things pertaining to God. This commandment seems ironic because Laodicea was famous for its ointments used for eye treatments and medicine for the eyes.

FACE AS A MAN – (Rev. 4:7) One of the creatures that surround the throne of God has a "face as a man," meaning that it is likely a glorified man.

FACES AS MEN – (Rev 9:7-11) The locusts seen by John that were released from the abyss represent or resemble something foreign to his time. Therefore

John uses vocabulary and metaphors with which he is familiar to describe what he sees in vision. The locusts may represent modern fighting vehicles or combat helicopters that had "faces as men" but had breastplates of iron, "hair of women," "the teeth of lions" and had the sound of "chariots . . . running to battle." It is even possible that John saw a major urban interstate congested with automobiles with the hapless faces of commuters, men and women, who serve the beast, peering out of the windshields. In short, the locusts represent a technology unleashed upon the world that is used by man to "hurt men."

FACE OF HIM THAT SITTETH ON THE THRONE – (Rev. 4:2; 6:16; 22:4) God the Father. **Face** is a word used idiomatically to connote personage, being, presence.

FACE OF THE SERPENT – (Rev. 12:14) The **woman** [symbolizing the Church] was delivered from the "**face** of the **serpent**" [referring to the presence of the **devil**] and was carried to the wilderness [representing a place of safety].

FALSE PROPHET – (Rev. 16:13; 19:20; 20:10) (Matt. 7:15; 24:24) The second beast that came "out of the earth." (Rev. 13:11-12) The **false prophet** is likely a person or a type for a particular kind of person who encourages the worship of the "beast" and represents all social, political and religious philosophies that stand in opposition to truth and the teachings of Christ. The **false prophet** appears to be part of an unholy trinity with the **dragon** and **beast**, all of which are given dominion over the earth in the **last days**.

FALSE TEACHERS/FALSE PROPHETS – *See* **Anti-Christs**.

FAMINE – (Rev. 18:8) (Hel. 11:4; D&C 43:25; 87:6) *See* **Hunger**.

FEAR – (Rev. 1:17; 2:10; 21:8) (D&C 63:17-18; 88:91) The opposite of faith; Believers are admonished to not fear "things which [they] shall suffer." We read in 2 Tim. 1:7: "God hath not given us the spirit of fear; but of power, and of love, and of a sound man." Those who fear and do not "**overcome**" are denied entry into the **New Jerusalem** and suffer the "second death." They who are kept out of the holy city, in this order, are "the fearful, and unbelieving, and the whoremongers, and sorcerers, and idolaters, and all liars."

FEAR GOD – (Rev. 14:7; 11:18) (Psalm 96:9; D&C 45:39) Respect, reverence God in a spirit of love and awe. *See* **Worship**.

FEET, UNDER/STANDING ON [or] IN – (Rev. 3:9; 7:1; 10:2,5,8; 12:1; 14:1; 19:1,17) Eph. 1:22; (D&C 88:110) Expression indicating dominion over that which is under the feet.

FELLOWSERVANT – (Rev. 19:10; 22:9) Brother in the gospel, including mortals, angels and resurrected beings; fellow laborers, companions in the ministry. President Joseph F. Smith clarified these passages in Revelation: "We are told by the Prophet Joseph Smith that 'there are no angels who minister to this earth but those who do belong or have belonged to it.' Hence, when messengers are sent to minister to the inhabitants of the earth, they are not strangers, but from the ranks of our kindred, friends, and fellow-beings and fellow-servants"

(Gospel Doctrine, p. 435).

FIG TREE/UNTIMELY FIGS – (Rev. 6:13) (Isaiah 34:4; D&C 88:87) Unripe, winter figs which appear early in the season, are generally weak, of poor quality and are easily knocked from the tree by wind gusts and during storms.

FIRE – (Rev. 3:18) (1 Cor. 3:13; 1 Peter 4:12) Instrumentality by which men will be tried and tested; (Rev. 4:5) Presence of the Holy Ghost is likened to fire; (Rev. 8:5; 9:17; 18:8; 20:9-10; 21:8) (Deut. 28:22; Mal. 3:2; Mark 9:43-44; 2 Peter 3:7) Means by which God will punish and destroy the wicked. Babylon the Great is to be burned by fire. Whether this is to be done literally or figuratively remains to be seen. There is scriptural basis to back those who believe that there is a location called hell, a place of everlasting burning and torment; (Rev. 15:2) (Isaiah 33:14) God dwells in the midst of everlasting fire. (Joseph Smith, TPJS, p. 367) *See* **Cloud.**

FIRE AND BRIMSTONE – (Rev. 14:10; 20:10) *See* **Brimstone.**

FIRE PROCEEDETH OUT OF THEIR MOUTH – (Rev. 11:5) The two witnesses in Jerusalem will have the power, as did the prophet Elijah (2 Kings 1:10-14), to call down fire from heaven to consume their persecutors.

FIRST HEAVEN, FIRST EARTH – (Rev. 21:2) The second estate, or the world we live in now in our mortal existence in this probationary state.

FIRSTFRUITS – (Rev. 14:4) (Jeremiah 2:3; 1 Cor. 15:20; D&C 88:97-98) Offering, sacrifice.

FIRST BEGOTTEN OF THE DEAD — (Rev. 1:5)

The first resurrected.

FIRST LOVE – (Rev. 2:4) Jesus Christ; This expression is reference to the Saints' original commitment and warmth which they felt when they were first converted to the Lord's gospel.

FIRST RESURRECTION — See entry under **Resurrection**.

FIVE [5] – Symbolic of something weak or incomplete but at the same time connotes God's grace and mercy. Man has five fingers and five toes on each hand and foot, respectively. Man is decisively weak and dependent on God's power to deliver. Man's power is insufficient and limited as is that of the devil. Jesus fed the multitude with five loaves of bread (John 6:9). Jesus died having suffered five wounds while on the cross (John 20:27).

FIVE MONTHS – (Rev. 9:5,10) Number of months occurring after the sounding of the fifth trumpet and are part of the first "woe" [possibly with the number five being used symbolically or literally], after the opening of the 7th Seal and before the Second Coming, during which the first universal plagues are unleashed upon the people of the earth and are represented by "**smoke of the pit**," **darkness,** and swarms of "**locusts**" and "**scorpions**"; These plagues will not kill, or exterminate mankind, but for five months they will torment "men which have not the seal of God in their foreheads." The smoke of the pit, the darkened sun, etc. clearly represent the launching of a ferocious assault of Satan upon the world to more fully establish his dominion and power. This will be done by lies, deceit, sorcery, and the seduction of men to his cause which is to make men miserable, corrupt, violent and self-serving. Most commentators and Church authorities suggest that the "locusts" and "scorpions" represent roving and rampaging armies which may have previously unleashed a type of warfare which has left the earth's environment and people "poisoned" and "tormented" but not dead, but the Lord limits them [the locust and scorpions] in their power and scope of destruction, hence the number "five"—denoting a confinement of duration, half of a whole.

FLAME – *See* **Eyes.**

FLOOD/WATERS OF THE RIVERS/OVER-FLOWING WATERS – (Rev. 9:14; 12:15) (Psalms 18:4; Isaiah 17:12-13; 43:2; Jeremiah 46:7-8) Imagery and language associated with massive military invasions, chaos, violent persecution and destruction. *See* **Waters as a Flood.**

FOOT – (Rev. 10:2) *See* **Feet.**

FOREHEAD – (Rev. 13:16-17; 14:1,9; 20:4; 22:4) *See* **Mark of the Beast** and **Seal of God.**

FORNICATION – (Rev. 2:14,20-21; 9:21; 14:8; 17:2,4; 18:3,9; 19:2) (Jeremiah 3:8; Ezek. 16:28-29; 2 Peter 2:3) Unlawful sexual relations outside of marriage. See **Adultery**; Apostasy, turning away from the truth; Worshipping false gods/idolatry [such as materialism]; Secret combinations and relationships established to get gain, power, wealth and recognition using any means possible including the influence and power of Satan and the agreement to secret oaths.

FORTY TWO [42] – (Rev. 11:2; 13:5) *See* **Three and a Half.**

FOUNDATIONS OF THE WALL [of the New Jerusalem] – (Rev. 21:14,19) The wall of the **New Jerusalem** will rest upon twelve **foundations**, each named after one of the "twelve apostles of the Lamb." These **foundations** are to be garnished with precious stones and gems. From a symbolic point of view the walls of the city will be founded upon the priesthood and teachings of the Apostles. It is also significant that each of the stones or gems in the foundation of the wall corresponds to gems on the breastplate of the high priests who officiated in the tabernacle during the time of Moses. In this latter case the gems stood for the twelve tribes of Israel.

FOUNTAIN – (Rev. 7:17; 21:6) (Psalms 36:8-9; Jeremiah 2:13) *See* **Water of Life.** (Rev. 8:8; 16:4) *See* **Waters to be Cursed**.

FOUR [4] – (Rev. 20:8) Reference to the four corners of the earth [geographically speaking]; Symbolic meaning of wholeness or completeness, universal.

FOUR AND TWENTY [24] ELDERS – (Rev. 5:8,14; 11:16) (D&C 77:5) *See* **Elders, Four and Twenty.**

FOURSQUARE – (Rev. 21:16) The **New Jerusalem** is to have four walls forming a square. The length, breadth and height of the city are equal, thus making the city an exact cube.

FOUR ANGELS – (Rev. 7:1) (D&C 77:8) Angels come from the presence of God and hold "power over the four quarters of the earth" (Joseph Smith, **TPJS**, p. 321). The angels are authorized to restore gospel truths, seal the righteous unto exaltation and are "waiting to pour out the judgments" of God "over

CLAY A. WESTOVER

the entire earth" (Wilford Woodruff, **JD**, Vol. 19, June 30 1878, also **YWJ**, 5:512); (Rev. 9:14) Four demonic angels that were set free to tempt man to war one with another.

FOUR BEASTS, in the midst of the Throne of God – (Rev. 4:6,8; 5:6,8,14; 6:1,6; 7:11; 14:3; 15:7; 19:4) These four living creatures [incorrectly translated from the original to 'beasts'] are of great symbolic importance. They exist in the form of creatures that have existed on this planet, other planets (D&C 77:2-3) or in Heaven. They serve as guardians at the four corners of the throne of God [implying geographical or locational significance as well]; (Rev. 4:7) The four creatures are the **lion, ox/calf,** a **beast like unto man** and a **flying eagle.** (Ezek. 1:10)

FOUR HORSEMEN – *See* **Horsemen, Four.**

FOURTH PART – (Rev. 6:7) Part or fraction of a whole. The portion of the earth given to the scourge and dominion of the **pale horse** and its rider, **Death,** was predetermined and limited.

FRANKINCENSE – (Rev. 18:13) Fragrant resin that is burned as incense.

FREE AGENCY/WILL – *See* **Agency/Free Will.**

FROGS – (Rev. 12:16; 16:13) Lies; (D&C 50:1-3) Unclean spirits that go forth to deceive and propagate the work of the devil, of the beast and of the anti-Christ. Synonym for a flood of lies; Words of false teachers; "**Frogs** come out of the mouth of the dragon, . . . the beast, and the . . . false prophet." This parallel construct stands as a contrast to the "**two-edged sword**" of truth which comes forth out the mouth of God (Exodus 8:2-7; Psalms 78:45;

105:30).

FRUIT, TWELVE KINDS – (Rev. 22:2) (1 Nephi 8:10-12) *See* **Tree of Life.**

FULFILLED/FILLED UP/FULL – (Rev. 15:1,8) Brought to completion.

FURLONG – One **furlong** is 1/8 of a Roman mile or approximately 607 English feet.

FURLONGS, ONE THOUSAND AND SIX HUNDRED – (Rev. 14:20) Expression that emphasizes the universal and all-encompassing magnitude of the destruction of the wicked. Sixteen hundred (1600) **furlongs** are just less than 200 miles.

FURLONGS, TWELVE THOUSAND – (Rev. 21:16) The width, breadth and height of the New Jerusalem are each 12,000 furlongs. This number is most likely symbolic and represents absolute wholeness of power and authority [represented by the number 12] multiplied by an inexpressible magnitude [represented by the number 1,000].

GARMENT – (Rev. 3:4-5; 16:15) (Isaiah 52:1; 61:10) Protective clothing that is symbolic of covenants made with our Heavenly Father. To keep one's garments can be interpreted with two meanings: 1.) Keep promises, especially as they pertain to the ordinances and sacraments of the Church; 2.) Be prepared for any of life's circumstances or eventualities.

GARMENT, DEFILED – (Rev. 3:4) (Alma 7:25)

Expression applied to those who violate covenants or have their raiment stained with the blots of sin. Those with **defiled garments** are left defenseless in a world of trial and temptation.

GATES – (Rev. 21:12-13,21,25) (Isaiah 60:11; Ezek. 48:31-34) The four-sided wall of the **New Jerusalem** will have twelve **gates**, three on each of the four walls. On each gate is inscribed one of the names of a tribe of Israel. Twelve angels stand guard over the gates in order to restrict entry into the city to those who are worthy to enter.

GIRT ABOUT THE PAPS – (Rev. 1:13) Wrapped around the chest.

GLASS – (Rev. 21:18,21) Synonym for Crystal. Probably an allusion to the pure, brilliant, illuminating and shining splendor of the **New Jerusalem**, not to mention the superior workmanship involved in its creation. *See* **Sea of Glass.**

GOD, THE FATHER – (Rev. 14:7; 22:9) He whom we worship in the name of His Son, Jesus Christ. He is both the literal physical and spiritual father of Jesus Christ and our spiritual Father (John 20:17). The purpose of this mortal life is to learn what we need to know and do in our current state of existence in order to return to God the Father and receive His "glory and dominion" (Rev. 1:6) (Dan. 7:14).

GOG AND MAGOG – (Rev. 20:7-8) (Ezek. 39:1,4; D&C 88:112-115) The forces of Satan that will rally to fight against the "camp of the saints" and the "beloved city." The battle of **Gog and Magog** will take place immediately following the Millennium, when the devil and his followers will be temporarily released from their "prison" and prior to the transformation of the earth into its celestial state.

GOLD – (Rev. 4:4) Twenty-four Elders sit around the **throne** of God. Each wears a "crown of **gold**," symbolic of the priceless gift of eternal life (Rev. 14:14); One "like unto the Son of man" wore a "golden crown," a symbol of royalty (Rev. 21:18,21). The **New Jerusalem** is described as resembling **gold**, which symbolizes the royal, eternal and enduring nature of this holy city (Rev. 3:18) (Isaiah 48:10; 1 Peter 1:7; Zech. 13:9); Saints are to become refined as **gold**, and "pass through the furnace of affliction" (Rev. 17:4; 18:12,16); Symbol representing the extravagance and indulgence of the **Whore** of **Babylon**.

GOLDEN GIRDLES – (Rev. 1:13; 15:6) Robes of the priesthood. Often used in the phrase with "**white linen**." The girdle itself probably consists of a belt and sash.

GOLDEN VIALS – (Rev. 5:8; 15:7) *See* **Vials/Bowls/Censers.**

GOOD/EVIL – (Rev. 12:1-17) (D&C 76:28-29) Our mortal existence on earth is a probationary state where the battle between good and evil continues, a struggle which started with the war in heaven between Satan with his agenda of compulsion, deceit, selfishness and lies and the plan of the Christ with the gifts of agency, free will, individuality, truth and priesthood (Alma 12:24; 34:32-33). The outcome of the choices we make on a daily basis and the effort we put into the battle will have eternal consequences for us individually, for our families, communities and the world.

GRACE – (Rev. 1:4; 22:21) (2 Thess. 2:16; James 4:6; 1 Peter 5:5) Strength and enabling power that a person derives from the unconditional love, mercy and kindness extended by Jesus Christ. Peter expresses it best: "Wherefore gird up the loins of your mind, be sober, and hope to the end for the grace that is to be brought unto you at the revelation of Jesus Christ" (1 Peter 1:13).

GRAPES – (Rev. 14:18) *See* **Cluster.**

GRASS – (Rev. 8:7; 9:4) On a literal level, fields of green grass represent sustenance for domestic animals and are viewed in a providential and positive light (Psalms 90:5-6; Isaiah 40:6-8; Matt. 13:38; 1 Peter 1:24; 1 Nephi 8:9,20). On a more figurative plane, the image of a vast field stands as a metaphor for the world in general. *See* **Green Thing.**

GREEN THING – (Rev. 9:4) (Job 15:32; Psalms 23:2; 37:1-2; 52:8; Jeremiah 11:16; Hosea 14:8; D&C 135:6) Color associated with life, hope and exaltation. Because grass, plants and the leaves of trees are green, this color has come to symbolize the vibrancy and renewal of life of man in particular (Rev. 8:7). So strong is this association that loss or destruction of "any green thing" is seen as a threat to the survival of man.

GUILE – (Rev. 14:5) Deception, deceit.

HAIL – (Rev. 8:7; 11:19; 16:21) (Ex. 9:18-26; Josh. 10:11; Ezek. 13:11-15; 38:22; D&C 29:16; 109:29-30)

Great hail storms have been a primary means by which the Lord brings His judgments upon the people of the world.

HAIR OF WOMEN – (Rev. 9:8) The locusts that torment the earth have "hair as the hair of women." Long hair may be an allusion to strength and manliness.

HAIR, WHITE – (Rev. 1:14) (D&C 110:3) The Lord is seen by John as having white hair which is consistent with the glory, wisdom and eternal character of Jesus whose "countenance shone above the brightness of the sun."

HALF AN HOUR – *See* **Silence in Heaven.**

HAND, RIGHT – (Rev. 1:16-17; 2:1; 5:7) (Isaiah 41:10,13) The hand of the Lord that upholds and sustains. It is the hand that is associated with the Lord's righteousness, power, salvation and justice. It is considered a great honor to be found at the "right hand" of the Lord (Psalms 17:7; 48:10; 89:13; 48:13; D&C 29:12); The hand with which covenants and oaths are made (Isaiah 62:8).

HARLOTS – (Rev. 17:5) *See* **Mother of Harlots.**

HARP – (Rev. 5:8; 14:2; 15:2) (Psalms 92:1-3) All who enter into God's presence receive this musical instrument with which to worship and praise God.

HARVEST – (Rev. 14:15) (Luke 10:2; D&C 4:4; 101:64-67) *See* **Reap.**

HEADS, SEVEN – (Rev. 12:3; 13:2) In chapter 12 Satan is portrayed as being a red dragon with seven heads. In the next chapter a beast in the likeness of Satan, in that it has seven heads, arises from the sea. (Rev. 17:9-10) The heads of the beast represent rulers who govern and control **seven mountains**, or nations and kingdoms of the earth.

HELL – (Rev. 1:18; 6:8; 20:13-14) (2 Peter 2:4; D&C 29:38) A word used usually in combination with or in context of 'death,' 'suffering' and 'separation;' Associated with both physical and spiritual death.

HIDDEN MANNA – (Rev. 2:17) Reference to the spiritual Bread of Life. As the manna sustained the Israelites until they reached the promised land, our acceptance of Jesus Christ as our Savior and our obedience to His teachings will sustain us on our journey to spiritual renewal and eternal life.

HOLD – (Rev. 18:2) Prison, ward, place of confinement. *See* **Cage.**

HOLD FAST – (Rev. 2:13,25; 3:3,11) (1 Thess. 5:21) Remain faithful. *See* **Endure well until the end.**

HONEY – (Rev. 10:9-10) (Psalms 119:103; Ezek. 3:3) The reception of God's word to the prophets is compared to the tasting of honey.

HOPE – (Lamentations 3:26) *See* **Endure well to the end**. John the Revelator was one of the most skilled prophetic writers in his ability to point out the discrepancies and contradictions between gospel ideals and the realities in today's mortal world. He clearly points the way to the ultimate source of our hope and trust. John fortifies our resolve and awareness by entrusting us with knowledge to comfort and to sustain us and help us to prepare for and withstand the present day and keep in remembrance the promises and blessings that await us in the future (1 Peter 1:13; 3:15; 1 John 3:2-3); *See* **Blessings for Righteous.**

HORNS, FOUR, of the Altar – (Rev. 9:13) Symbolic

of the safety and sanctuary to be found in God's tabernacle and in true religious worship.

HORNS, SEVEN – (Rev. 5:6) Joseph Smith was inspired to change the number "**seven**" to "**twelve**" in this verse, which indicates that the **twelve horns** represent the fullness of priesthood power of Christ (Psalms 75:10; 112:9).

HORNS, TEN – (Rev. 12:3; 13:1; 17:3,7,12,16) (Dan. 7:20,24) Ten very wicked, violent and corrupt rulers or leaders, regimes, or powers that gain power in **Babylon**. The **seven kings**, represented by the **seven mountains** and the **seven heads** of the beast, eventually lose power and dominion over the world resulting in chaos, self-destruction, and war. As usual Satan abandons his followers and these servants of the devil that brought **Babylon**/the **whore** to her height of notorious glory in the first place (1 Nephi 22:13; Alma 30:60). They turn on each other and spare no effort to destroy any obstacle to their insane, selfish lust and appetite for recognition, power and wealth/material gain. In the process they destroy **Babylon** and bring the eternal **Wrath of God** upon the planet. [Note again that we may not necessarily take the numbers "seven" and "ten" as literal numbers. Their use may be symbolic.]

HORNS, TWO – (Rev. 13:11) The creature with **two horns** is described as being a "second beast" which arose from the land, a deformed lamb, or a false Christ. His master is the devil and he reinforces the power over the "first beast" [the spiritually depraved powers of Babylon/the whore] as well as its heads and horns [the worldly, physical kingdoms of men].

HORSE[S] – Large four-legged hoofed domestic beast of burden used to transport goods and people. There is no record of the Israelites routinely domesticating the horse until the reign of the Kings, at which time [about 1000 B.C.] David and Solomon took in horses from Egypt and trained them to perform in battle (1 Kings 4:26; 10:26; Job 39:19-24). Because of their speed, intelligence, strength and endurance, horses have been widely employed throughout the history of most cultures to carry mounted warriors into battle, or pull chariots and/or carriages. (Rev. 9:7,17) The horses of the great armies that gather upon the earth in the last days may be interpreted as being armored vehicles that have "heads of lions" and inflict death upon man by breathing out "fire, smoke and brimstone" (Rev. 19:11,14,19,21). At His coming in glory Jesus and His "armies in heaven" will be mounted upon **white horses** in a mighty display of power, majesty and righteousness. Isaiah makes mention of horses being used for agricultural purposes, namely, threshing grain (Isaiah 28:28). The symbolism of the horse may vary from culture to culture, tradition to tradition, but generally the horse is a symbol of strength, virility and masculinity.

HORSEMEN, FOUR, [of the Apocalypse] – *See* explanation under **Seals**. The four horsemen of the Apocalypse appear in John's vision as the first four seals are broken on the scroll with seven seals in Chapter 6 of John's Revelation; Like other images of the Apocalypse, the **four horsemen** have been the subject of much speculation, imagination and fascination, mainly because of their association with the "end of the world" and the mystery surrounding their identities. John never writes explicitly who they are, what they represent, where they came from and what purpose they serve. We only get clues from the colors of the horses, the historical context, and the appearance of the riders. *See* **White**, **Red**, **Black** and **Pale**.

HORSE BRIDLES – (Rev. 14:20) In John's view of the destruction of the wicked in the "winepress of the wrath of God," the blood overflowing the press is to reach such a depth so as to submerge the bridles on the horses. This may be John's way of saying that the profusion of blood will be so great as to be very deep. Another possible explanation for this phrase is that John foresaw a great battle in the vicinity of Palestine that was so violent that blood literally filled the valleys to a great depth.

HOUR, ONE — See **One Hour**.

HOUR OF HIS JUDGMENT – (Rev. 9:15; 14:7) Appointed time at which God will execute His punishing curses/plagues and judgments upon the wicked of the world.

HOUR OF TEMPTATION – (Rev. 3:10) Any time of trial or temptation; Prophetically speaking it is the final great tribulation when God pours out his wrath and judgments upon the world.

HUNDRED, FORTY AND FOUR CUBITS – (Rev. 21:17) The measure of the wall that surrounds the **New Jerusalem**. Since that makes the length of the wall a multiple of twelve, the number represents a fullness of priesthood authority.

HUNDRED AND FORTY AND FOUR THOU-

SAND [**144,000**] – (Rev. 7:4; 14:1,4-5) (D&C 77:11; 133:18) Selected servants of God the Father who will "follow the Lamb whithersoever he goeth" and who will be preserved during the tribulations and afflictions of the last days in order to help believers in Christ escape Babylon and the ensuing chaos that will engulf the world. This number is not to be taken literally. It represents the redeemed and chosen of the Lord.

HUNGER – (Rev. 6:8; 7:16; 18:8) (Isaiah 49:9-10) Hunger and famine give rise to powerful images of suffering and are viewed as punishments from God. Freedom from hunger and thirst are seen as evidence of God's power to save.

HUSBAND – (Rev. 21:2) *See* **Bridegroom.**

$-\mathcal{C}^{\mathcal{Q}}_{\mathcal{J}}-$

IDOLATRY – (Rev. 2:14; 2:20; 9:20-21; 18:4-19; 21:8) (Psalms 115:4-8; Jeremiah 45:5; 2 Nephi 9:30; D&C 1:16) Perversion of the knowledge and worship of the true God, supplanting them with the worship of, lust for, and the desire for the acquisition/control of worldly powers and material substance; Spiritual fornication. Influence exercised over wealth, fame, technology, the fruits of others' labors, and the means of production, distribution of worldly goods for profit and gain at any cost. Any other relationship engendered for the accomplishment of the same; Isaiah, Jeremiah and John the Revelator consistently condemn the fascination with, the preoccupation with and the reliance on "the works of our hands" and the "arm of flesh." Idolaters are mentioned as being a class of people destined for the "lake which burneth with fire and brimstone." *See* **Fornication**.

INCENSE/VIALS OF ODORS – (Rev. 5:8; 8:3-4) (Ps. 141:2) Prayers of the saints.

INDIGNATION – (Rev. 14:10) (D&C 43:26; 88:88) Extreme displeasure, used as a synonym for "**wrath**."

IRON – (Rev. 2:27; 12:5; 19:15) (Psalms 2:9; 1 Nephi 11:25) "**Rod of iron**" is the law/word of God.

ISLAND, EVERY – (Rev. 16:20) Distant lands, faraway countries.

IVORY — (Rev. 18:12) Symbol of beauty and luxury.

-*J*-

JACINTH – (Rev. 9:16-17; 21:20) Red-brown form of zirconium silicate; Gem/precious jewel included in the foundation of the wall of the **New Jerusalem**; Found on the high priest's breastplate.

JASPER – (Rev. 4:3; 21:11,18-19) (Ezekiel 28:13) Red, yellow, brown, green opaque variety of **chalcedony**, a precious and valuable stone that is as crystal and very brilliant (Ex.28:20; 39:13); Sometimes rendered as moonstone. The glory of God and of the **New Jerusalem** is as elegant and exquisite as **jasper**.

JESUS CHRIST – *See* **Atonement of Jesus Christ**.

JESUS CHRIST, Names and Titles of – (Rev. 1:1, 8; 11:15; 14:12; 19:1; 22:21) In the book of Revelation the Lord Jesus Christ is referred to by almost fifty different titles, names and appellations, each of which symbolize, describe, or characterize His role, sovereignty, mission, stature, and/or destiny in the Eternal scheme of things:

He who is, was, and is to come—(Rev. 1:4; 1:8; 4:8, 10; 11:17; 16:5) Title that declares His eternal existence; the name Jehovah comes from this expression as do the names and titles **Alpha and Omega, the beginning and the end**—(Rev.1:8,11; 21:6; 22:13), **the beginning of the creation of God**—(Rev. 3:14), **the First and the Last**—(Rev. 1:11,17; 2:8; 22:13), **Endless and Everlasting**—(Moses 1:3; 7:35; Helaman 13:38; Isaiah 9:6; D&C 19:12)

Him who loved us, Him who washed us from our sins—(Rev. 1:5)

The Lord Omnipotent, Lord Almighty, Almighty [God]—(Rev. 1:8; 4:8; 11:17; 15:3; 16:7; 19:6,15; 21:22); **Lord God**—(Rev. 18:8); **the living God**—(Rev. 7:2)

Prince of Kings of the earth—(Rev. 1:5), **King of Kings,** and **Lord of Lords**—(Rev. 17:14; 19:16) (1 Tim. 6:15); **King of Glory**—(Psalms 24:7); **King of the Jews**—(Matthew 2:2); **King of Zion** (Moses 7:53); **King of saints**—(Rev. 15:3); **Lord of Lords**— (Rev. 17:14; 19:16)

Hidden manna—(Rev. 2:17)

Amen—(Rev. 3:14)

The bright and morning star—(Rev. 2:28; 22:16)

Faithful and True [Witness]—(Rev. 1:5; 3:14,17; 19:11; 21:5)

Holy and True—(Rev. 3:7; 6:10)

Father—(Rev. 1:6); **God**—(Rev. 1:1) [Used 83 times in the book of Revelation as applying to Jesus.]

God who lives forever and ever—(Rev. 4:9; 10:6; 15:7)

He who was dead, and is alive—(Rev. 2:8)

The first begotten of the dead—(Rev. 1:5)

Word of God—(Rev. 1:2; 19:13)

Rod/Root [and offspring] of David—(Rev. 5:5; 22:16) (Isaiah 16:5; Jeremiah 23:5)

Son of Man—(Rev. 1:13; 14:14) (Acts 7:56); **Son of God**—(Rev. 2:18)

Lion of the Tribe of Judah—(Rev. 5:6)

Lamb—(Rev. 5:6) [This reference to Christ is used at least 28 times in the book of Revelation.]

God of Heaven [and] Earth—(Rev. 11:13-14) (Isaiah 44:6-8; 45:18)

JEZEBEL – (Rev. 2:20,24) Name of [or figurative reference to] a false prophetess that resided at **Thyatira** during John's ministry. She encouraged fornication and idolatry. (1 Kings 16:31-33) The Jezebel in John's day and the Jezebel, evil wife of King Ahab, in ancient times serve as types for the downfall of the whore Babylon. In the same way that Jezebel fell from the window and was devoured by the dogs, the great harlot described by John the Revelator will fall and be devoured by the beast, which afterwards will turn upon itself in acts of self-destruction (Rev. 17:16).

JOHN THE DIVINE – The author of the book of Revelation (Rev. 1:1,4,9; 22:8); The Beloved Apostle; Son of Zebedee; "Son of thunder;" Apostle of the Lamb; Brother of James; "flaming fire;"

"ministering Angel" (D&C 7:6; 3 Nephi 28:6-7).

JUDGMENT – (Rev. 20:4,12) The right or power to rule, preside, minister to, plead in behalf of; During the final judgment, the books will be open and all will be judged by the words, thoughts and deeds recorded in those books, therefore, to a large degree each will be his own judge and have a perfect knowledge that God's actions are just (Alma 41:7-8); Judgment, or punishment of the wicked, comes as a consequence of remaining unrepentant (Rev. 16:11; 19:2) in order for the demands of Justice to be met.

JUDGMENTS AGAINST THE WICKED – (Rev. 1:7; 2:23; 21:8; 22:11) *See* **Tribulation**; The punishing judgments of God that come after man has been warned to repent, be it by His Spirit, prophets, teachers, or tribulation (D&C 88:88-91); The divine destructive judgments of God in the final days of the earth's temporal existence will not only bring about final repentance and deliverance from the Beast and the Anti-Christ, but also the final and ultimate destruction of the wicked and the purification of the earth itself (Mal. 3:5); Once the wicked realize their day of reckoning has arrived, many will cry out to the rocks, "Fall on us, and hide us from his [God's] presence." (Rev. 6:16) (Alma 12:14) All men, including "the kings of the earth" to "every free man," will be filled with terror when "the great day of [God's] wrath is come" (Rev. 6:15-16). The judgments are carried out according to prophetic pronouncements, are based on the deeds and works of men in the flesh and have been described in the scriptures as being "never-ending torment, a lake of fire and brimstone, whose flame ascendeth up forever and ever and has no end" (Rev. 14:11; 20:13-15) (Isaiah 24:5-6; Heb. 10:30-31; 2 Peter 3:7; D&C 43:29; 76:31–46; Mosiah 2:37,39; 2 Nephi 9:15–16; 3 Nephi 10:14).

JUDGMENT, FINAL – (Rev. 16:8-11; 20:11-15) All people, without exception, will stand before God to be judged in the context of a final judgment or undergo an assessment of words, thoughts, deeds and accomplishments while in the flesh. Accountability will be expected and consequences will real, immediate, just and immutable. (John 5:22) The Father has given the right to judge the world to His Son, whose judgments will be done "in righteousness" (Psalms 19:9; Isaiah 11:4; Matt. 25:14–30; Romans 2:6-8,16; 14:12; 2 Nephi 9:11-12,15,46; Alma 29:3,6; D&C 128:6-8).

KEEP/KEPT – (Rev. 3:10) Observe, maintain; Preserve, give refuge to. Protect, guard.

KEY[S] – (D&C 65:2) *See* **priesthood**; Symbols of authority/priesthood, access and jurisdiction; Keys may be delegated, permanent or temporary. In specific context, keys represent the authority of God to perform assigned tasks and duties. Keys cannot be randomly, arbitrarily transferred or abused because of the sacred nature of the callings within the priesthood; Right, power and ability to control and rule over. For example, Christ holds the "keys of hell and of death" (Rev. 1:18).

KEY OF DAVID – (Rev. 3:7) (Isaiah 22:22) The right to occupy the throne of David and rule over Israel as her rightful king.

KEY OF THE BOTTOMLESS PIT – (Rev. 9:1; 20:1-3) The right and authority to use divine prerogative to contain or release the powers of hell and evil that dwell in the "**bottomless pit**."

KEYS OF HELL AND DEATH – Christ holds "the keys of hell and death" (Rev. 1:18) and exercised them by entering the spirit world to preach to those who rejected Noah and the prophets. Jesus holds the keys over the grave and the spirit world. The Apostle Peter greatly expands the scope of that work, saying that all are accountable before God for their stay in mortality and that "for this cause was the gospel preached also to them that are dead" (1 Peter 4:6).

KINDREDS, TONGUES, PEOPLES AND NATIONS – (Rev. 5:9; 7:9; 10:11; 11:9; 13:7; 14:6; 17:15) (D&C 77:11) Peoples, multitudes of the earth.

KINDREDS OF THE EARTH – (Rev. 1:7) Families of the earth, tribes of the earth (Matt. 24:30); Peoples in each of their various stations in life on earth (Rev. 6:15; 13:16; 19:18).

KINGDOMS OF THIS WORLD ARE BECOME THE KINGDOMS OF OUR LORD – (Rev. 11:15; 19:19,21; 20:9) (Isaiah 60:11-12; Jeremiah 30:11; Dan. 2:44; 7:9,14, 27-28; Zech. 14:9; 1 Cor. 15:24; D&C 41:4; 84:118; 87:6; 105:32; 133:25) At the height of their power over the world, Christ will personally intervene to destroy the beasts and the nations of the world, including their wicked rulers. The righteous will reign with Jesus upon the earth and the **Resurrection of the Just** will begin.

KINGS OF THE EARTH – (Rev. 16:14; 17:2; 18:9)

Rulers of the nations and economies of the world. (Rev. 21:24,26) The **kings of the earth** that bring their "splendor and honor" to the **New Jerusalem** are NOT the former rulers in the fallen world. They are the righteous individuals, servants, and martyrs, who through the grace and mercy of their Heavenly King, are worthy to enter the **Holy City** and bring their eternal reward with them (Rev. 1:6).

KINGS OF THE EAST – *See* **East.**

KNOWLEDGE – During the Millennium, the knowledge of God and Christ will prevail upon the earth (2 Nephi 30:16-18; Isaiah 11:9; 54:13; Jeremiah 31:34; Hab. 2:14; Hebrews 8:10-11). To the degree that light and truth permeate the souls of man at that time, the glory of the earth's inhabitants will shine above the glory of the sun, moon and stars (Rev. 21:23-26; 22:5) (Isaiah 60:19-20). Contrast these previous images now with the words of Amos 8:11-12 and Isaiah 5:13 which describe the state of a people in darkness and apostasy, a people at a great distance from Christ.

LAKE OF FIRE AND BRIMSTONE – (Rev. 19:20; 20:10,14-15; 21:8) (Dan. 7:11; 2 Nephi 9:16) The ultimate fate that awaits the "beast," the "false prophet [Anti-Christ]," the fearful, the unbelieving, murderers, whoremongers, sorcerers, idolaters, liars and all who love and make a lie. The Prophet Joseph Smith stated: "A man is his own tormentor and his own condemner. Hence the saying, They shall go into the lake that burns with fire and brimstone. The torment of disappointment in the mind of man is as exquisite as a lake burning with fire and brimstone. I say, so is the torment of man" (**HC**, 6:314). *See* **Brimstone**.

LAMB OF GOD – (Rev. 5:6,12-13; 7:14,17; 12:11; 13:8; 14:4; 17:14) (John 1:29) The Holy Son of God, Jesus Christ; The Lamb stands as a symbol [of a divine sacrifice] in contrast to the Dragon, Satan. It is the "blood of the Lamb" that cleanses the saints, ensuring their victory over Satan.

LAMP – (Rev. 4:5) Alternate translation for **Candle/Candlestick**.

LAODICEA – (Rev. 1:11; 3:1) Town in a Roman province in Asia Minor known for its commercial, scientific, medical, financial and manufacturing industriousness; It had a small community of saints to which John wrote an account of his Revelation; these saints were known for being attentive to their secular enterprises and business ventures, but were distracted and less than enthusiastic about their commitment to the gospel and were labeled as being "lukewarm" and therefore they would be rejected by the Lord for their lack of dedication to Him.

LAST DAYS – (Rev. 1:1; 4:1; 22:6-7) (D&C 77:13; Ether 4:16; 1 Nephi 14:22) The "last days" is a term which generally refers to a period of time that comes just before the end of the mortal telestial world as we know it, prior to the Second Coming of Jesus Christ. When compared with the age of this world it is a relatively short period of time during which many dramatic, sensational and eternally defining events will take place, events which will increase in intensity and frequency as the time approaches for the Son of God to return in glory. It is a period of time unnecessarily cloaked and shrouded in mystery and misunderstanding. There is no end to the speculative discussions among both Christians and non-believers regarding what is widely regarded as the "end of the world." Nevertheless, inspired prophets, both ancient and modern, make clear what is in store during this period of time:

There will be a restoration of the fullness of the gospel of Jesus Christ which will be accompanied by the coming forth of revelation, scripture, prophecy, priesthood and an increase of faith and knowledge concerning the things of God (Rev. 14:6-7) (2 Nephi 26:16-17; Isaiah 2:2-5; Dan. 2:27-28,34-35,44; D&C 10:46-47; 45:9; 65:2).

All manner of miracles, signs and wonders will occur: natural and man-made disasters and phenomena will abound; There will be miracles performed by faithful men and women of God in the name of Christ and for the good of man. Miracles will also seemingly be caused by individuals who are under Satanic influence and/or by means of unseen forces that stand in opposition to God (Matthew Chapter 24; D&C Section 88 and D&C 45:36-40).

During the last days there will be revelation and inspiration provided by God to encourage man to build up the Kingdom of God and to prepare mankind for the "end of the world" and the coming of Jesus Christ, keeping in mind that God has never revealed when His Son will return in glory and power. Even though we may not live or expect to live to see the ushering in of the millennial peace, if we live in a manner worthy of a millennial people, our children and future generations will be blessed for our efforts and the Lord will be pleased with them when He comes. They will have sufficient knowledge, understanding, and spiritual maturity to recognize and welcome their God (Rev. 5:13) (Isaiah 25:8-9; 54:13; D&C 130:1-2). The opportunities to build Zion and to prepare are rapidly passing us by (Alma 34:32-33; Alma 37:47; Helaman 3:35).

Men will become unrepentant (Rev. 9:21) (Jude 1:16,18-19; 2 Peter 3:3-4), self-sufficient and proud, boasting that "I am rich, and increased with goods, and have need of nothing" (Rev. 3:17).

The Lord's people will drift into apostasy (Rev. 13:1-18). (Daniel 7:21) In the last days the "beast" will become overwhelming and "power will be given unto him to make war with the saints, and to overcome them . . ."

Satan will have great power in the last days, fear will overcome many, but those who refuse to worship the image of the beast and Satan, (Jeremiah 51:6) and flee **Babylon**, will ultimately triumph. A millennial reign of peace will ensue (Rev. 20:1-6; 21:4-8) (Isaiah 54:17; 2 Nephi 28:19-20; D&C 45:36-40).

As the latter-day work comes to a close the following events will indicate the ushering in of the Millennium:

All wickedness will come to an end and Babylon [meaning the world and its wickedness] will be overthrown. Satan will be bound for 1,000 years (Rev. 16–18) (Isaiah 63:1–6; 1 Nephi 22:26; D&C 88:110; 101:24).

Zion will be established in the earth and Jesus will reign in the midst of his Saints (1 Nephi 22:14-20; D&C 1:36; Moses 7:60-64).

All political kingdoms and nations will come to an end and Jesus Christ will become the King of Kings who rules over all the earth (Rev. 11:15) (Zech. 14:16–17; D&C 87:6).

The world will enter a millennial era of peace, harmony, righteousness, bounty, learning and advancement (Isaiah 65:17-25; D&C 101:26-34).

LEAVES OF THE TREE WERE FOR THE HEALING OF NATIONS – (Rev. 22:2) (Ezek. 47:12) The leaves of the **Tree of Life**, which stands as a symbol for the love of God, administer relief and healing in this life if we avail ourselves to their use. In the same way that man extracts essential nutrients and medicinal compounds from the leaves of trees, so may man make beneficial use of the leaves of the **Tree of Life**. The image of leaves providing protection and relief may also be expressed more simply in terms of shelter for birds and their nestlings, and of shade for man seeking relief from the heat of the **sun**.

LEOPARD/LEOPARDESS – (Rev. 13:2) (Daniel 7:6) The first "beast" [rendered by Joseph Smith as "image/sign/likeness unto/of a beast"] arises from the sea and is in the form of a leopard, with feet as a bear, a mouth of a lion. This beast receives power and dominion from the Dragon and represents the evil, corrupt, and degenerate earthly nations, kingdoms, and societies that will dominate the world in the last days. Chronologically this "beast" comes to power at some point shortly after John receives the vision itself and after the true Apostles of Jesus Christ perish from the earth. The beast reigns upon the earth until the Lord and select servants return in glory to obliterate any and all vestiges of this corrupt creature. Many modern commentators think that John had the Roman Empire in mind when using the symbol of the leopard, and that the other animals mentioned by John represented either empires in existence at his time or prior to it (Isaiah 11:6; Jeremiah 5:6; 13:23; Hos. 13:7; Hab. 1:8). Of all of God's creatures, the leopard is proportionately stronger than any other animal and has the most powerful jaws of any animal alive. It can kill and carry prey that triple the leopard in weight and size; Throughout all cultures and traditions, the leopard, though generally not linked to deity, is associated with the world of the spirits because of its graceful, elusive, evasive, solitary, and cunning nature, possessing mystical and mysterious powers from an unseen world, thus instilling fear in man and beast alike throughout the ages. Hosea and Jeremiah use the leopard to symbolize God's wrath. The words "leopard" and "lion" are used in similar contexts, but are not used interchangeably.

LIGHT/TRUTH/INTELLIGENCE – (Rev. 21:23-24; 22:5) (Isaiah 60:19-20) The Glory of God, qualities which inherently characterize Jesus Christ and His Father. They are so intense in magnitude that the glory thereof exceeds the sun, moon and stars and will serve as the light of the **New Jerusalem** where there will be no distinction between day and night because of the presence of the Son of God. Compare with **Candlestick**.

LIGHTNINGS AND THUNDERINGS AND VOICES – (Rev. 4:5; 8:5; 11:19; 16:18) (Job 37:3-5; Psalms 18:12-14; 77:18; D&C 43:21-22,25; 88:88-92) Expression that portrays God's control and power over all creation. *See* **Voices**.

LIKE UNTO – (Rev. 1:13; 14:14) Expression that identifies the entity that is seen, heard or perceived; Perception of the similitude of an object, "as" (Dan. 3:25; Abr. 3:27).

LINEN, CLEAN AND WHITE – (Rev. 15:6; 19:8,14) Clothing worn by the angels in the presence of God; Righteousness of the Saints who will be prepared as a '**bride**' that awaits the '**bridegroom**'. *See* **White Robes**.

LION[S] – (Rev. 4:7) One of the beasts which stands guard at the throne of God; (Rev. 9:8; 10:3; 13:2) Various beasts mentioned in the Revelation have the heads and/or mouths of lions; (Numbers 2:3) The lion serves as the symbol of the insignia of the tribe of Judah (Gen. 49:9) which was to settle on the east side of Palestine "toward the rising of the sun." Traditionally the lion has been known in all cultures and traditions for its power, strength, courage, and royal nobility. The roar of the lion is meant to mark its territory and instill fear in its occupants. (Joel 1:6-7) Lions have been used in prophetic writings to represent anciently the powerful empires that ruled the world at the time, such as Assyria and Babylon.

LION OF THE TRIBE OF JUDAH – (Rev. 5:5) Jesus Christ. Title referring to His power, might and dominion.

LIVING WATER – *See* **Water of Life**.

LOCUSTS – (Rev. 9:3,7) (Ex. 10:12-15; Psalms 78:46; 105:34; 109:23; Proverbs 30:27 Isaiah 33:4; Joel 1:4; 2:25) The depiction of swarms of **locusts** conjures up images of recurring or seasonal plagues. In modern times such plagues of **locusts** may be interpreted as being a metaphor for war, terrorism, bigotry, economic crises, and debilitation caused by chronic sickness. During the plagues of **locusts** man is tormented but not destroyed. It is likely that "**locusts**" and "**scorpions**" are any and all emissaries, demonic converts, agents or instruments in the hands of the devil.

LOOSE THE SEALS [of the Book] – (Rev. 5:2) (Phil. 2:9-10) No angel in Heaven nor man on earth was worthy to open the book containing the history of the world. Only the Lamb that gave Himself as a sinless sacrifice, invested with power from His Father, was authorized to unseal the great scroll.

LORD'S DAY/DAY OF THE LORD – (Rev. 1:10) (Isaiah 2:12; 13:6; Joel 2:1-2,11; Amos 5:18; Obadiah 1:15; 2 Peter 3:10; D&C 128:24) Sunday, Sabbath Day; Judgment Day, not necessarily the Sabbath Day given the context, purpose and nature of this eschatological work. "The day of the Lord is great and very terrible; and who can abide it?"

LUCIFER – (Isaiah 14:12-16) *See* **Satan**.

LUKEWARM WATER – (Rev. 3:15-16) Water that is not cold and cannot satisfy the thirst of the laborer and traveler, nor is it warm or hot for washing and healing. Therefore, it is only good to be "spewed out of the mouth." This term is used as a metaphor to describe saints who lack commitment or faith, or are otherwise indifferent, apathetic or complacent to the matters of the spirit (Rev. 3:19) (D&C 76:79).

-*M*-

MAN CHILD – (Rev. 12:5) Christ's church, the political kingdom and government of God on earth, Zion; Jesus Christ.

MANNA, HIDDEN – *See* **Hidden Manna**.

MARK OF THE BEAST – (Rev. 13:16-18; 14:9,11; 15:2; 16:2; 19:20; 20:4) Those who wish to prosper in the world receive the mark of the beast upon their foreheads and right hand. This mark signifies that both loyalty and labor will be devoted to the work of the **beast**. The mark is to be contrasted with the seal/name which is placed upon the foreheads of those who follow the Son of God. The "mark" may be literal or figurative in nature and any attempt to identify it is speculative (Rev. 7:3; 9:4; 14:1); (Rev. 15:2) Allusion to anything that is evil, including the works of the devil.

MARBLE — **(Rev. 18:12)** Symbol of wealth, luxury, and nobility. Its presence is associated with palaces and temples.

MARRIAGE – (Rev. 19:7) *See* **Bride/Bridegroom**.

MARRIAGE FEAST/SUPPER OF THE LAMB – (Rev. 19:7-9; 21:2) (Isaiah 25:6; Luke 14:7-24; D&C 58:7-11; 65:3) The union of the Lord [the Groom] and the earthly Church, or Zion, and the New Jerusalem and City of Enoch, is depicted as a joyous marriage and feast between the Lord and His people [the Bride]. The marriage feast of the Lamb is symbolic of the reign of Christ to come during the Millennium. The **Bridegroom** is Jesus. The **Bride** is the Church/Zion/Israel, or in other words, the saints collectively. The clean white linen is representative of the sanctified, pure and holy status of the **Bride**. In some accounts of the marriage feast there are guests mentioned which may be a representation of the worthy Saints individually that sit and sup with the Lord. *See* **Bride/Bridegroom**.

MATERIALISM/WEALTH/SELFISHNESS/BABYLON – (Rev. 3:17-18; 18:2-17) Cause for fall of Babylon and destruction of the world. (D&C 29:21; 88:94; Alma 30:17; 1 Nephi 22:23; 2 Nephi 9:50-51; Mormon 8:34-40) The most troubling form of idolatry that John foresees in the last days is that man will predominately trust most in "the works of his hands" and in "the arm of flesh." Material possessions, money and wealth constitute the false gods of our day. Gaining wealth, merchandising, consolidating economic power, gaining possessions, consuming goods and services in accordance with lust and envy, exploiting the labor and will of others, and blatant concupiscence will characterize the citizens of Babylon at the height of their wickedness.

MEASURE OF WHEAT/ MEASURES OF BARLEY – (Rev. 6:6) During the period of time covered by the third seal, characterized by the rider of the black horse of the Apocalypse, life would be plagued by famine. It would require an entire day's wage to buy enough **wheat** and **barley** to survive from day to day.

MEASURE [the Temple/Altar/Them that Worship] – (Rev. 11:1) Symbolic act of specifying that which is to be placed under God's protection. The temple and altar may refer literally to the latter-day temple to be built in Jerusalem (1 Cor. 3:16; 2 Cor. 6:16; Eph. 2:19-21). The word "**temple**" is also a metaphor for individual persons. (D&C 101:11; 109:45) Measuring may be another way of expressing the way in which the "**seal of God**" will be placed upon those to be protected from the "**wrath of God**" when it is "poured out upon the wicked without **measure**." (D&C 1:10) **Measure** may carry with it the connotation of **judgment**; (Rev. 21:15-17,22) (Job 38:4-7; John 2:19; D&C 1:9) This act of measuring the temple is strikingly similar to a vision of Zechariah in which a young man is seen measuring Jerusalem in preparation for the city to be possessed again by the children of Judah. (Zech. 1:16; 2:1-5,12) Jesus referred to His own being as a *temple*. The measurements spoken of here may be a standard that is set by the Messiah Himself and none other. The **New Jerusalem** has no *temple* "for the Lord God Almighty and the Lamb are the *temple* of it."

MERCHANTS – (Rev. 18:3,11,15,23) Those who prospered and controlled the economies of the world during the reign of Babylon. The lavish and opulent lifestyle of the merchant class is revealed symbolically by the manner of goods in which they traded. They would commerce in luxury items such as "gold, and silver, and precious stones" as well as "fine linen, purple, and silk and scarlet."

MICHAEL – Adam; Known in the latter-days as Michael, the archangel, chief angel, seventh angel. He stands next to Jesus Christ in priesthood and authority as pertaining to Heavenly Father's children (Rev. 12:7) (Dan. 10:13; 12:1; Jude 1:9; D&C 27:11; 29:26; 78:16; 88:110-112).

MILLENNIUM – (Rev. 20:1-7; 21:4,6) (Moses 7:64; Isaiah 11:6-9; 65:17-25; Ezek. 34:25-31; D&C 29:11; 43:30; 45:58–59) Also referred to as **The First Resurrection/The Resurrection of the Just**. The Millennium is a time that is to be characterized by beauty, peace, rest (Isaiah 14:7), priestly people, a terrestrial order of government, truth, and the physical presence of the Son of God. Satan will be bound and have no power over the people who live during the Millennium for a space of 1,000 years.

MILLSTONE, CAST INTO THE SEA – (Rev. 18:21-22) (Jeremiah 25:10) A "mighty angel" will cast a "great millstone" into the depths of the sea. With this gesture we are to learn that Babylon will be "thrown down, and shall be found no more at all." **Babylon** will no longer serve as a center for worldly pleasures, economic activity nor industry.

MIRACLES – (Rev. 12:9; 13:13-14; 16:13-14; 20:3,8) (Matt. 24:24) Deceivers and spirits of devils are able to work miracles and perform wonders. They will be so convincing that they will persuade the "kings of the earth" to gather their armies together to battle; *See* **Last Days**.

MIXTURE, WITHOUT – *See* **Without Mixture**.

MOON – (Rev. 12:1) Representative of a glory or eternal reward less than the glory of the sun. Since the moon reflects light and does not radiate it, the moon may, figuratively speaking, be representative also of falsehood, counterfeit or imitation. It is therefore very significant that the woman clothed with the sun is standing upon the moon, thus manifesting eventual power and dominion over all man-made religions and philosophies.

MOON BECAME AS BLOOD – (Rev. 6:12) (Joel 2:31; Acts 2:20; D&C 29:14; 34:9; 45:42; 88:87) The moon will not likely literally turn into blood. In the same manner that the sun will refuse to give its light, the moon will appear to turn as red as blood. The phrase may be used figuratively to reflect the prevailing conditions [such as abnormal weather phenomena] and circumstances [such as war] upon the earth.

MORNING STAR – (Rev. 2:28; 22:16) (1 Peter 1:19) Jesus Christ; The promise that the righteous will receive the "**morning star**" may be a reference to the privilege and hope of obtaining the Second Comforter [or personal visitations from Jesus Christ] in this life or to a promise of the glory of the Son in the life to come.

MORTALITY/PROBATIONARY STATE – *See* **Good/Evil**.

MOTHER OF HARLOTS – (Rev. 17:5) (1 Nephi 14:16-17) **Babylon**; In the same manner that disciples of Jesus emulate the Master, **Babylon** encourages and inspires her followers to sin and perform wicked and evil works. Babylon engenders and fosters any fraternal or social organization, religion, government, philosophy, practice or movement that are false and designed to lead men astray and estrange them from the true

God.

MOUNT SION/ZION – (Rev. 14:1) (Psalms 48:2; Isaiah 4:5; 8:18; Joel 2:32; Obadiah 1:17; D&C 76:66; 133:18,56) Holy place; Mount of Olivet, location to which the glorified Lord will return to the earth to save and reign over His people; (Isaiah 24:23; D&C 84:2) City of the **New Jerusalem**; (Isaiah 18:7; Heb. 12:22) Gathering place for the Lord's elect.

MOUNTAIN/ISLAND MOVED/FLED – (Rev. 6:14; 16:20) Expressive description of how the earth will return to its primal condition and be prepared for the ushering in of the Millennium.

MOUNTAIN[S] – (Rev. 16:20) Nations, countries.

MOUNTAIN[S], HIGH – (Psalms 87:1; Isaiah 2:2-3; Joel 3:17; Zech. 8:3) Holy place, Temple; Location where God reveals His will to His prophets (Rev. 21:10) (Ezek. 40:1-2; 1 Nephi 11:1; 2 Nephi 4:25; Ether 3:1; Moses 1:42).

MOUTH – (Rev. 1:16; 12:15; 13:2) From a figurative point of view the mouth is the organ or agency through which a process or endeavor is put into motion. From a literal point of view God's purposes are accomplished by the word of His power. By extension, the will of the Lord might be made known through the Lord's mouth, or mouthpiece, known as a prophet or Apostle. The devil also has something to say and speaks through his demonic emissaries. The second beast, or false prophet, appeared to be a lamb but "spake as a dragon" (Rev. 13:11).

MYSTERY – (Rev. 17:5) One of the names of **Babylon**, a name assumed in order to mock the

Lord who returns with a "name written that no man knew (Rev. 19:12). **Babylon** would have us believe that God is unknowable and unknown, that man is basically left on his own without the means or ability to know God. Man is thereby persuaded to abandon the gospel and its ordinances for material-istic and worldly pursuits, the gratification of which is more tangible and immediate.

MYSTERY OF GOD – (Rev. 10:7) (Eph. 1:9; 3:3-5; 6:19; 1 Nephi 10:19; Alma 12:9; D&C 42:61; 76:7; 77:6) Knowledge that is only available through reve-lation from God to specified servants at the time and in a manner appointed by God.

NAKED – (Rev. 3:16) Even though people profess otherwise, God sees past appearances; (Rev. 16:15) If a person were to lose his **garments** he would be exposed, improperly attired and left vulnerable or defenseless. *See* **Garments**; (Rev. 17:16) **Babylon** will be made "desolate" and stripped of her outward ornamentation and attractiveness and revealed for the counterfeit and imposter that she is. The beauty and attractiveness of **Babylon** is only superficial in nature.

NAME, NEW — *See* **New Name**.

NATIONS – *See* **Kindreds, Tongues, Peoples & Nations**.

NEW – (Rev. 21:5) (D&C 101:25) As contained in the Lord's declaration, "Behold I make all things new," this term suggests there will be a regeneration of the fallen world, redemption of man and a transition from all former things to a more elevated spiritual plane and a newness of existence.

NEW EARTH/NEW HEAVEN – (Rev. 7:15-17; 21:1) (Isaiah 65:17; 2 Peter 3:13; Ether 13:9; D&C 29:23-25; 88:18-19) The celestialized earth, the habitation destined for the redeemed saints and their God; State of existence characterized by no evil, no death, no mourning, no tears, no sorrow, and end to suffering. Final judgment/justice will have occurred and all will have entered into their appropriate degree of glory.

NEW JERUSALEM – (Rev. 3:12; 21:2,10—22:5) (D&C 45:65-71) Referred to as just "Jerusalem" by the earlier prophets; A literal city which will exist during the Millennium. It stands as a virtuous "maiden" in contrast to the telestial whore **Babylon**; (Isaiah 54:11; 60:10-14; Haggai 2:7-9; Zech. 2:1-5; 9:9-10; Moses 7:62-63; Heb. 11:16) The appearance and description of the city and its wall is likened to precious gems and has streets of gold (Rev 21:11-23); The **New Jerusalem** is not only to be considered a central place of gathering and the administrative center of the Saints in the Millennium, but by extension the **New Jerusalem** is synonymous with the word **Zion** and stands as a symbol for all the habitations of the Saints and includes the Ten Tribes, the City of Enoch, the Stakes of Zion, etc.

NEW NAME – (Rev. 2:17; 3:12) (Isaiah 44:5; 62:2; Mosiah 5:7) Name of Jesus Christ which we receive after baptism; Reference to the covenant making process, where the **new name** becomes a key word or password (D&C 130:11); Symbolic of a new beginning or major change or event in life, such as marriage, birth, priesthood ordinances, bestowal of special office or calling.

NEW SONG – *See* **Song, New.**

NICOLAITANS – (Rev. 2:6,15) (D&C 117:11) Early Christians who adhered to a Greek philosophical heresy that advocated no need for a moral code and condoned sensuality. It advocated that sins of the flesh had no relation to one's spiritual being, since the physical and spiritual creature are two separate and distinct parts of the same person. Therefore sins of the body had no influence on the condition or destiny of the person's spirit in eternity.

NIGHT — (Rev. 8:12; 21:25; 22:5) Used both literally and figuratively to denote darkness, doom, tribulation and absence of the Spirit.

NO MORE – (Rev. 3:12; 7:16; 18:14,21-23; 20:3; 22:3) Statement declaring that one reality, that of the world, is replaced by another, the heavenly.

NO MORE CURSE – (Rev. 22:3) The curse the Lord pronounced upon the earth at the time of Adam's fall will be removed.

NOISOME – (Rev. 16:2) Repulsive, disgusting, foul.

NOUGHT/NAUGHT – (Rev. 18:17) Nothing, in vain, of no consequence.

NUMBERS/NUMEROLOGY, SYMBOLISM OF – John the Revelator uses numbers, multiples of numbers and numerical expressions extensively after a pattern established by prophetic writers in the Old Testament and he does so in order to make his writings meaningful only to those who are attentive and spiritually alert. Numbers used may symbolically represent:

Wholeness, completeness, perfection, totality;

Priesthood, holiness, godliness, governance, royalty;

Imperfection, deficiency, continuing cycles, a part of a whole, counterfeit or evil;

Superlative expression, greatness of magnitude.

-Ø-

OCEAN – *See* **Waters**.

ODOURS – (Rev. 5:8) Incense.

OF JESUS CHRIST, REVELATION – (Rev. 1:1) The use of the word "of" could be interpreted in three ways: 1.) *about*, referring to content; 2.) *from*, referring to source; and, 3.) *belonging to*, referring to possession or ownership of.

OIL AND WINE, HURT NOT – (Rev. 6:6) Expression used in parallel with wheat and barley. States that God places a limit on the adversary's ability to destroy the basic needs of man, thus ensuring man's survival.

OLIVE TREES – Because an olive tree represents an investment that spans generations before it becomes truly productive, the olive tree is symbolic of the Lord's long-term and eternal plans, purposes and designs for His people Israel; Olive oil is such a precious commodity in ancient Israel, that the fruit of the olive tree is a metaphor for the anointing of royalty or the preparation and divine calling of a prophet.

OLIVE TREES, TWO – (Rev. 11:4) (Zech. 4:11,14) The two special witnesses spoken of in Chapter 11 of John's Revelation are likened to "two olive trees." *See* **Witnesses**.

OMNIPOTENT – (Rev. 19:6) *See* **Almighty**.

ONE [1] – (Rev. 18:8) Oneness, unity; Inseparable, indivisible.

ONE DAY – (Rev. 18:8) (Isaiah 10:17; 47:9; D&C 64:24) Babylon will be destroyed as it were in **one day**, overnight and not a single part of her will be spared destruction.

ONE HOUR – (Rev. 17:12; 18:10,17,19) From an eternal perspective **Babylon** and the **kings** of the earth will dominate the world for a relatively short time and then Babylon's destruction will come suddenly as if in **one hour**. It is noteworthy that the fall of Babylon is witnessed **three** times by **three** groups of people who have been her primary benefactors: "the kings," "the merchants of the earth" and "every shipmaster and sailor." Her demise will be swift, thorough and irreversible.

OVERCOMETH – (Rev. 2:7,11,17,26; 3:5,12,21; 21:7) (1 John 4:4-5) To be born of God and become one of His sons or daughters, to undergo a spiritual rebirth. The prescription for "**overcoming**," as found in Rev. 12:11, is: 1.) Acknowledge the shedding of the blood of the Lamb of God, and be washed clean by it; 2.) Possess the gift of prophecy and testimony; 3.) Love God and the Lamb more than one's own life; and, 4.) Rejoice and express thanksgiving. *See* **Endure Well to the End**.

OX /CALF – (Rev. 4:7) One of the "beasts" that guards the throne of God; A creature known for its strength, endurance and capacity to perform work. The economies of entire communities depended on the people's skill at breeding and caring for their calves and oxen. The **ox** is the symbol or the insignia of Ephraim's ensign that was to be planted in the west. (Numbers 2:18)

–⟨ℰ⟩–

PALE [or **PALE GREEN**] – (Rev. 6:8) The color of the fourth horse of the Apocalypse. Pale green suggests death, despair, and relentless pestilence.

PALM [BRANCHES] – (Rev. 7:9) (Matt. 21:8; John 12:12-13 D&C 109:76) Symbol of joy and triumph. **Palm** branches are traditionally waved and cast at the feet of royalty, nobles and conquering heroes.

PARADISE – (Rev. 2:7) (Luke 23:43; 2 Cor. 12:4) The abode of just souls where "the spirits of those who are righteous are received into a state of happiness, which is called paradise, a state of **rest**, a state of peace, where they shall rest from all their troubles and from all care, and sorrow" (Alma 40:12). *See* **Rest**.

PATIENCE – (Rev. 1:9; 2:2-3; 2:19; 3:10; 13:10; 14:12) Luke 12:19; (Rom. 15:4-5; Heb. 6:12; 10:36; 1 Thess. 5:14; James 1:3-4; 5:7-8; 1 Peter 2:20; D&C 54:10; 101:38) *See* **Endure well to the end**.

PATMOS, ISLAND OF – Island located in the Aegean Sea about fifty miles southwest of Ephesus that served as a place of exile for criminals and enemies of the empire (Rev. 1:9–19).

PEACE AND CONSOLATION – (Rev. 7:16-17; 21:4) (Isaiah 26:3; 54:13, Philip. 4:7) The most significant blessing of living during the Millennium is the blessing of living when peace and harmony will reign upon the earth. Personal inner peace comes as a result of the comfort we receive from the Holy Ghost as we strengthen our faith in Jesus Christ [a major reason for John's recording of the Revelation in the first place]. We learn the will of God and perform it according to the best of our understanding. We endure in prayer, study, faithfulness, service and good works and *it* [the inner peace] is a blessing we are privileged to enjoy here and now during the trying and tiring preparations we are making to meet our God (1 Cor. 14:3).

PEARL – (Rev. 21:21) Material of which the gates of the New Jerusalem are made; The image of the **pearl** may refer to the shape of the gates to the **New Jerusalem** The pearl is also symbolic of God's truth and refining influence.

PEARLS – (Rev. 17:4; 18:12,16) Used as a symbol representing the extravagance and excesses of the **whore Babylon**.

PENNY – (Rev. 6:6) A day's wage.

PEOPLES – *See* **Kindreds, Tongues, Peoples & Nations**.

PERSECUTION – (Rev. 1:9; 2:3,9-10,13) One of the many trials and tribulations suffered by the early saints. We learn from the first chapters in the book of Revelation that the Apostle John was well aware of afflictions of the saints, apostasy and dissension within the Church. John recorded this magnificent Revelation to serve as a comfort to the saints that the Lord ultimately controls the powers of evil and that great blessings will be found awaiting those who **overcome** and **endure well unto the end**.

PERDITION – (Rev. 17:8,11) (D&C 76:31-38) Eternal damnation, everlasting spiritual death.

PERGAMOS – (Rev. 2:12-17) City located in Asia Minor, present day Turkey, where the saints suffered severe persecution since it was a center for pagan worship after the manner of the Greeks as well as the site of a prominent Roman establishment for higher learning. The saints here indulged in some carnal and sensual heresies which displeased the Lord. John called them to repentance or else they will face destruction. If they do repent, they will grow in knowledge of God and receive His love and approval.

PERSONAL REVELATION – *See* **Spirit of Revelation**.

PHILADELPHIA – (Rev. 3:7-13) City in Asia Minor, which had only a small, weak, but faithful and courageous congregation of saints who suffered ruthless persecution at the hands of the local Jewish community. The Lord promises them through John that He would deliver them from temptation and reward their patience with a crown of glory. The saints of Philadelphia and Smyrna were the only congregations not rebuked by the Lord.

PIERCED HIM – (Rev. 1:7) (Zech. 10:12; 13:6; John 19:34-37; D&C 45:51-52) Reference to the crucifixion and the piercing of Jesus' side with a spear by the Roman soldier.

PILLAR OF THE TEMPLE IN HEAVEN – (Rev. 3:12) (Gal. 2:9) Symbolizes strength and stability; Status and destiny of redeemed priesthood holders who have overcome the world and will serve the Lord in His temple in the hereafter.

PIT, BOTTOMLESS – (Rev. 9:1-2,11; 11:7; 17:8; 20:1,3) (Num. 16:33) Hell, the dwelling place of the **devil**; (Psalms 9:15; 35:7; Proverbs 28:10) Satan's trap or snare, devilish devices which are often laid by man and take captive those who set them; (Psalms 40:2) Term that describes any deep trial or trouble; Literal captivity from which there is no escape.

PLAGUE[S] – (Rev. 15:1,6,8; 16:1-21; 18:4,8; 22:18) (D&C 5:18-19) Great affliction or distress, especially one of divine retribution; Sudden outbreak of something, such as a disease. *See* **Curses**.

POOR – (Rev. 3:17) Lacking in matters as pertaining to the spirit.

POTTER — (Rev. 2:27) (Isaiah 64:8) The **potter** stands as a type for the Lord who molds and fashions man according to His designs and wisdom.

POWER – *See* **priesthood**.

PRAYER – (Rev. 3:20) Jesus Christ answers prayers (D&C 6:14-15; 88:63; Isaiah 58:9-11; 65:24; Jeremiah 33:3).

PRECIOUS STONES – (Rev. 17:4) Along with **gold** and **pearls** the harlot Babylon adorns herself with precious stones, a blatant display of her vanity and materialistic appeal. (Ex. 28:17-21; Isaiah 54:11-12) Anciently precious stones, representing the twelve sons of Jacob, were found on the breastplate of the high priest. The foundation of the wall of the New Jerusalem is adorned with precious stones that are associated with the Twelve Apostles. (Rev. 21:19-20) The stones comprising the foundation of the New Jerusalem's wall are the following: jasper, sapphire, chalcedony, emerald, sardonyx, sardius, chrysolite, beryl, topaz, chrysoprasus, jacinth, and amethyst.

PREMORTAL LIFE – *See* **Satan, Premortal Existence** (Rev. 12:4) (D&C 29:36; Moses 4:3-4).

PRIESTHOOD/KEYS/AUTHORITY/POWER – (Rev. 1:6; 3:7; 5:10; 9:1; 20:1,6) (Isaiah 22:22; 61:6; Eph. 2:19–20; 4:11–14; Luke 10:1; Acts 14:23; 1 Tim. 3:1, 8; 1 Peter 2:9) Priesthood is the power and authority God/Jehovah used/uses to create the world[s] and maintain order in his creations. Like Truth, priesthood is an eternal reality and stands independent within its own sphere and is a real and tangible force. Priesthood is the authorization conferred on man by God/God's servants to act in His name and perform whatever service or act He [God] should require. John makes reference to God's servants as being kings and priests (Rev. 5:10; 20:6). The Prophet Joseph Smith wrote: "Those holding the fullness of the Melchizedek Priesthood are kings and priests of the Most High God, holding the keys of power and blessings" (History of the Church 5:555). *See* **Key[s]**.

PRIESTS – *See* **priesthood**.

PRINCE OF THE KINGS OF THE EARTH – (Rev. 1:5) Jesus Christ.

PRISON – (Rev. 2:10) (Isaiah 61:1) Conditions or circumstances that deliver one, temporally or spiritually, to the temptations and buffetings of the devil; (Rev. 20:7) The dwelling place of the devil.

PROPHECY – (Rev. 1:3; 10:11; 22:7,10,18-19) The book of Revelation is identified as a "**prophecy**." *See* **Spirit of Revelation**.

PUNISHMENT – *See* **Judgments against the wicked**.

PURPLE AND SCARLET – (Rev. 17:4; 18:12,16) (Ex. 26:1; Lament. 4:5) The harlot **Babylon** is arrayed in these colors to demonstrate her pretentious wealth, nobility and royalty. **Purple** and **scarlet** are the colors of the curtains or veil that surround the **Ark** of the Covenant. Purple is not only the color of royalty, it is also associated with priestly office. **Babylon** not only endeavors to be the dominant political and social system of the world, but she portrays herself as an alternative religious system as well, mocking the true religion of Jehovah.

QUEEN – (Rev. 18:7) (Isaiah 47:7-11; Zeph. 2:15) **Babylon** the Great fancied herself to be a powerful royal **queen** that ruled the world by committing **fornication** with the **kings** of the earth. Her pride and arrogance prevents her from ever seeing that all her relations are illegitimate and there will be an end to her reign and glory, and that she would soon become desolate and a "widow."

QUICKLY – (Rev. 2:5,16; 3:11; 22:7,12,20) (D&C 1:35; 33:18; 34:7,12; 35:37; 39:24; 41:4; 49:28; 68:35; 87:8; 88:126; 112:24; 133:2) As in "I come **quickly**" means suddenly, speedily, unexpectedly, with no warning, when we least expect it, without a chance to prepare. It is interesting that John the Revelator opened the Apocalypse with these words that portray a sense of urgency: "The Revelation of Jesus Christ, which God gave unto him [John], to show unto his servants things which must *shortly* come to pass" (Rev. 1:1; 22:20). The faithful are reminded that they must be vigilant, watchful and repentant in order to be saved for the Lord will come as a "**thief**" in the night. The Lord warns us not to become complacent and lulled into thinking that "He delayeth His coming . . . ." For the day of His coming is indeed "even at the doors" (Rev. 3:3) (Mark 13:35-37; Luke 21:34-35; Matt. 24:37-38;

D&C 45:26; 110:16).

-ℛ-

RAIMENT – (Rev. 3:5) *See* **White Robes.**

RAINBOW – (Rev. 4:3) (Ezek. 1:28) A rainbow like unto an emerald surrounds the throne of God invoking a brilliant image of natural beauty, glory and attractiveness. (Rev. 10:1) A rainbow also crowns the head of the "mighty angel" symbolizing his glory and power. The emerald is a gem which traditionally represented the tribe of Judah; The color of emerald green is associated with life; (Gen. 9:13) The rainbow is a sign of a covenant between God and man suggesting that there must be a balance between mercy and justice.

REAP – (Rev. 14:15-16) (Hosea 6:11; Matt. 13:24-30; D&C 6:3; 86:1-7) To cut and gather in the harvest. In one sense the gathering of God's elect is a harvest; In another sense reaping means the death and destruction of the wicked (Jeremiah 51:33; Joel 3:13-14).

RED – (Rev. 6:4; 12:3) Color of the second horse of the Apocalypse and of the Dragon. Symbolizes war, bloodshed, wrath of God and sin; (Rev. 19:14) (Isaiah 63:1-3; D&C 19:18; 133:46-51) Christ will return to the earth wearing **red** apparel that will appear as though it were dipped it blood.

REED, [GOLDEN] – (Rev. 11:1; 21:15-16) (Ezek. 3:3,5) Measuring rod that is six **cubits** in length. [Six cubits is almost 10 feet]. See **Measure.**

REINS – (Rev. 2:23) (Job 16:13; Psalms 7:9; Isaiah

11:5; Jeremiah 11:20; 17:10; 20:12) Used in phrases such as "God searcheth" or "trieth the heart and reins." **Reins** is understood as being the mind, thoughts or understanding of man.

REMNANT – (Rev. 11:13; 19:21) Part that remains, residue.

REPENTANCE/GOD'S FORGIVENESS – (Rev. 2:5,20-21; 3:15) John's magnificent vision obviously occurred before he wrote the introductory chapters to the book of Revelation which are basically short messages or prefaces to the seven churches in Asia. Each individualized message contains five distinct parts:

1) A salutation or greeting in the name of the Lord and statements as to the authorization he has to represent the Lord Jesus Christ, whom he describes using many different titles and names;

2) Commendation for good works that they are engaged in, both as individuals and as a religious community, and expressions of support, sympathy or encouragement as necessary;

3) A strong rebuke or admonishment for wrong-doing, sins, or shortcomings;

4) A call to repentance and corrective action;

5) Promises of blessings are made in the name of the Lord to the degree that the Saints obey the commandments, repent and continue in the faith.

This prophetic formula is not unlike the revelations that the Prophet Joseph Smith pronounced to individuals and groups in the latter-days. Compare Revelations 2:4-6 to D&C, Section 117:11—Bishop Newel K. Whitney was earlier severely chastened by the Lord through the Prophet Joseph, as recorded in D&C 93:50. D&C 93:49 states: "What I say unto one I say unto all; pray always lest the wicked one have power in you, and remove you out of your place." This verse alone summarizes the purpose and intent of John's letter being sent to only seven of the churches since the conditions and situations in existence in those seven congregations of Saints are representative of those existing in all the Christian communities, both ancient and modern. In effect, John's message of the need for repentance and encouragement is indeed a message to all. *See* **Blessings for the Righteous.** When the call to repent is heeded and the humble Saints continue to pray, demonstrate faith and patience, and wait upon the Lord, the reality of the cleansing power of the Atonement becomes evident in the sinner's life (Isaiah 1:16-18; 43:25; Ezek. 18:21-22,31-32; 33:11,16).

The Lord will provide ample time for the wicked to repent before His coming in glory. As outlined in Revelation 6:12-15 and summarized again in similar wording in Doctrine and Covenants, Section 88:87-91, there will be many signs and wonders performed to warn the wicked that their time of judgment is approaching: 1.) Earthquakes 2.) Sun will become black; 3.) Moon will be turned to blood; 4.) Stars will fall from heaven; 5.) Heaven will roll as a scroll; 6.) Mountains and islands will be moved out of their places; and 7.) Fear will come upon all men. Amazingly, many will survive the plagues and will "repent not to give [God] glory" (Rev. 16:9).

REST – (Rev. 14:13) (Isaiah 14:7; Alma 40:12) State of calm and peace that will exist among the deceased of the Lord's Saints as it is written: "Blessed are the dead who die in the Lord, for they rest from their labors and their works do follow them." The exact opposite, a state of anxiety, commotion, fear and agitation will prevail among those who "worship the beast" (Rev. 14:11).

REST, LORD'S – For the concept of *rest* to be relevant and applicable, it must be available for man's enjoyment both in this life and the life to come. Please consider the following two quotes on the subject, one from a modern day prophet and the other from John's Revelation. "The ancient prophets speak of *'entering into the rest of God;'* What does it mean? That we are not hunting for something else. I pray that we may all enter into God's rest—rest from doubt, from fear, from apprehension of danger, rest from the religious turmoil in the world; from the cry that is going forth, here and there—lo, there is Christ; lo, here is Christ, lo, He is in the desert, come ye out to meet Him. The man who has reached that degree of faith in God that all doubt and fear have been cast from him, he has entered into *'God's rest.'* To the faithful Latter-day Saint is given the right to know the truth, as God knows it; and no power beneath the celestial kingdom can lead him astray, darken his understanding, becloud his mind or dim his faith or his knowledge of the principles of the gospel of Jesus Christ" (Pres. Joseph F. Smith, **CR**, October 1909, pp.3-9). "For the Lamb which is in the midst of the throne shall feed them, and shall lead them unto living fountains of waters: and God shall wipe away all tears from their eyes" (Rev. 7:17; 14:13; 21:4) (Psalms 116:7-9; Isaiah 25:8; 32:17-18; Alma 12:34-

35; D&C 42:46).

REST, NO [REST] DAY OR NIGHT – (Rev. 14:11) (Isaiah 57:20-21) The fate and lot of those who serve and worship the **beast** is to suffer exhaustion, anxiety and pangs of guilt in this mortal life of endless cycles of labor, gain and consumption in service to the god of materialism. Their eternal reward is that of the damned. "The sleep of the laboring man is sweet, . . . but the abundance of the rich will not suffer him to sleep" (Eccles. 5:12). *See* **Materialism**.

RESTORATION OF THE GOSPEL – (Rev. 10:11; 14:6-7) (D&C 77:9-10; 14; 88:103-104) Following a long period of apostasy the "everlasting gospel" was restored through the Prophet Joseph Smith by way of visions and ministering of angels. John the Revelator was commissioned to continue preaching "before many peoples, and nations, and tongues, and kings" and to play an important role in the Restoration of the gospel in this last dispensation (Rev. 6:12 to 7:17) (Isaiah 29:13-14; Daniel 2:44; Micah 4:1-2; Mal. 4:5-6; Acts 3:19-21; D&C 77:8; 88:103-104; 133:17,36-37). *See* **Last days**.

RESURRECTION – (Rev. 11:11-12) The two martyred prophets in Jerusalem are resurrected marking the end of the second "**woe**," just before the sounding of the seventh trumpet and the beginning of the third "**woe**;" (Rev. 20:12-13) (D&C 88:16) The resurrection is universal and the spirits and bodies of all mortals will be again united and all the dead will arise from the earth and from the bottom of the seas to give an accounting for their words, thoughts and deeds.

RESURRECTION, FIRST [OF THE JUST] – "Blessed and holy is he that hath part in the first resurrection: on such the second death hath no power, but they shall be priests of God and of Christ, and shall reign with him" (Rev. 20:3-7,11-12) (John 5:28–29; Rom. 8:17-18; 1 Cor. 15:22–23; 1 Thess. 4:16-17; D&C 29:13; 43:18; 76:50-70; 88:97-98). *See* **Millennium**.

RESURRECTION, SECOND [OF THE UNJUST] – (Rev. 20:5,13-15) (D&C 43:18; 76:32; 88:31-32; 101-102) "The rest of the dead lived not again until the thousand years were finished." Those who merit a glory other than that of celestial or terrestrial will not resurrect until after the Millennium.

REVELATION – *See* **Spirit of Revelation**.

REVELATION, MODERN-DAY – Many readers of the book of John's Revelation experience great confusion over the verses Rev. 22:18-19, which state that no one has the right to "take from" or "add to" *this book*. Readers assume that the authority and teachings of God are all self-contained in the Bible and that there is no need for on-going and continuing revelation from God to man. This line of thinking defies logic and denies our identities as literal spirit children of our Father in Heaven (D&C 1:4,17; 20:32-35). Never has there been a greater need for the children of God to receive [and listen to] revelation from God than now.

REWARD – (Rev. 11:18; 18:6; 22:12) (Isaiah 35:4; Heb. 11:6) Recompense; Divine gifts bestowed upon individuals as a consequence of living a life in harmony with righteous principles. Reward may also be negative, that is, a punishment inflicted for ungodly behavior.

RICH – (Rev. 2:9; 3:17) True wealth is to be found in being spiritually self-sufficient and not in being rich according to the materialistic world, for "he that hath eternal life is rich" (D&C 6:7).

RIGHT HAND – *See* **Hand, Right**.

RIPE – (Rev. 14:15,18) (D&C 29:9) Ready, fully developed.

RIVER[S] – (Rev. 8:10; 16:4) (Psalms 72:8; Isaiah 8:7; Hab. 3:5-8,12; Zech. 9:10) Synonym for **Sea[s]** and **Waters**. Symbolic of barriers or boundaries such as the protected borders of nations, or populated outposts. Scriptural references to curses upon the **Rivers** may also signify the prophesied "full end of all nations" (D&C 87:6).

RIVER EUPHRATES, DRIED UP – (Rev. 16:12) (Isaiah 11:15; 44:27; Jeremiah 51:36; Zech. 10:11) The drying up of rivers and bodies of water represents God's deliverance on some occasions, but in other instances it is symbolic of God's removal of His protective powers. In this case of the **Euphrates** becoming dry, the Lord is removing the barriers to the enemies of Israel and making Jerusalem vulnerable to attack.

RIVER OF WATER OF LIFE – (Rev. 22:1) *See* **Water of Life**.

ROBE[S] – (Rev. 6:11; 7:9) *See* **White Robes**.

ROD OF IRON – *See* **Iron**.

ROOT AND OFFSPRING OF DAVID – (Rev. 5:5; 22:16) (Isaiah 53:2) Jesus Christ.

_𝒮_

SACKCLOTH – (Rev. 11:3) Type of coarse, loose-fitting dark clothing that is usually made of goat or camel hair. It is a type of clothing associated with prophets. (Job 16:15; Psalms 35:13; Isaiah 37:1; Jeremiah 4:8; Dan. 9:3) The wearing of **sackcloth** implies a feeling of sorrow, mourning and grief.

SACRIFICE, ETERNAL NATURE AND POWER OF CHRIST'S – (Rev. 5:6,9-13) Through vivid images, symbols, and references, John the Revelator commits to the reader of the book of Revelation an insightful glimpse at the definitive majesty, glory and regency of the Lamb, as well as His resolute determination to perform the will of the Father at all times. And in doing so, John gives hope to the faithful. The Lamb, who sacrificed all, deservedly earns the praise and thanksgiving of the believers, not to mention their love, confidence and loyalty (John 3:16; 1 John 4:19; 2 Peter 3:9).

SALVATION – (Rev. 12:10) (Psalms 27:1; 118:14; Isaiah 12:2; 25:8-9) Redemption from the Fall, restoration to an immortal state of existence, through the grace and Atonement of Jesus Christ. Salvation encompasses all of God's children [except perdition] *and* all of His creations.

SALVATION, TEMPORAL – (Rev. 3:20-21; 7:9-17; 21:6-7) Salvation is a word often associated with spiritual rescue. The word "ransom" is associated with securing physical safety, which is often the way in which Isaiah refers to salvation by describing those who escape from Babylon as being ransomed or a remnant (Isaiah 35:10); Any effort to strictly define these words will become increasingly more difficult as the inhabitants of the earth begin to enter and live during the Millennium. In other words, if one does not repent as the final judgments come in rapid succession, with great severity, those very judgments will be to the eternal condemnation of the sinner (Rev. 14:9-11; 22:11-12) (2 Nephi 28:1-32; Helaman 13:13-14). Those who have fled **Babylon** and have repented will be comforted and protected during this time of cleansing (Helaman 5:23-24; 3 Nephi 17:24). *See* **Deliverance**.

SAND OF THE SEA – (Rev. 13:1; 20:8) Synonym for **stars**, children of our Father in Heaven. (Gen. 22:17) Descendants of Abraham.

SAPPHIRE – (Rev. 21:19) (Ezek. 1:26; 28:13) Brilliant and radiant blue variety of corundum; Precious stone used in the foundation of the wall of the **New Jerusalem** (Isaiah 54:11-14).

SARDINE/SARDIUS – (Rev. 4:3; 21:20) (Ex. 28:17; Ezek. 28:13) Precious stone found in the foundation of the wall of the **New Jerusalem**; The brilliance of God sitting upon His throne is described as being as **jasper**, that is, clear and brilliant, and **sardine** which is blood-red, crimson.

SARDIS – (Rev. 3:1-6) City located north of **Ephesus** and south of **Thyatira**. It was home to the Roman temple dedicated to Diana, the goddess of hunting, love and fertility. The economy relied heavily on the textile industry. The saints of this community had a reputation for being alive spiritually but were actually very weak, but the Lord expresses His awareness and feelings for the few remaining worthy and pure saints in **Sardis**, who are promised that they shall be clothed "in white raiment," their names will not be "blotted out of the book of life," and the Lord will "confess [their names] before the Father, and before the angels."

SARDONYX – (Rev. 21:20) Form of **agate** or **onyx**. Precious stone included in the foundation of the wall of the **New Jerusalem**.

SATAN – (Jude 1:6; Moses 4:3-4; D&C 29:36; 76:28; 2 Nephi 2:18; 9:9; Mosiah 16:3) Satan and his followers were cast out of heaven in the premortal life because of their rebellion against Heavenly Father. (Rev. 3:9; 12:7-9; 16:14; 20:7-8) From the original Greek word for *adversary* and Hebrew for *spoiler*; (Rev. 20:1-4) (1 Nephi 22:26; D&C 43:31) Satan is bound and rendered powerless for a thousand years during the Millennium. At the end of the Millennium, Satan will be loosed for a season, and he will gather up the wicked "in the four corners of the earth, Gog and Magog," to battle the righteous before the end of the earth and the final Judgment Day (Rev. 20:7–10) (D&C 88:110–16).

SATAN, PREMORTAL EXISTENCE AND WAR IN HEAVEN – (Rev. 12:3-17) (Isaiah 14:12-14; Moses 4:1-4; Dan. 10:13; 21:1; Luke 10:18; Abr. 3:27-28; D&C 29:36-37; 76:25–27) A common complaint of the modern age is that there is so much evil and hurt in the world today and people do not understand why a just God won't remove it outright. Little do they understand the eternal nature of the conflict between Satan and the Lamb, between Good and Evil, and that there are eternal laws such as agency, choice, responsibility, and accountability which existed prior to this life, that are in full force in mortality and are inseparably connected to our eternal destinies as we progress in our journey to return to our Father in Heaven and become like Him.

SCARLET – (Rev. 17:2-4) Synonym for **Red**. Color associated with life, death, sin, blood and violence of war. From a social point of view, **scarlet** is associated with wealth, upper class and nobility. The **whore Babylon** arrays herself in **scarlet** and **purple** in deceitful imitation of pretended royalty and sits upon a **scarlet**-colored **beast**, or **dragon,** which symbolizes **Satan**.

SCORPIONS – (Rev. 9:3,5,10) (Deut. 8:15; Ezek. 2:6) Metaphor describing evil men who have the power to inflict pain and suffering [the stings]. The scorpions are compared to the swarms of locusts unleashed by Satan to torment man.

SCROLL, HEAVEN DEPARTED AND ROLLED TOGETHER – (Rev. 6:14) (Isaiah 34:4; Mormon 9:2) The rolling together of the heavens as a **scroll** seems to be the reverse image of the breaking of the seals and unrolling of the booked sealed with seven seals which revealed the history of the world. Figuratively speaking the rolling of the heavens as a **scroll** suggests that the story of the world is finished, the earth is to transition from its mortal sphere to an exalted one. The glory of God is soon to be openly revealed and His judgments to be executed upon the world.

SEA – (Rev. 7:2-3; 13:1; 17:15) (Moses 7:66) *See* **Waters**.

SEA, NO MORE – (Rev. 21:1) (D&C 133:24) An expression indicating that all the earth's land mass and waters have returned to their original state as existed at the time of creation; The prophesied "end to all nations" (Jeremiah 30:11) has come to pass. God and his servants have established dominion over the earth. There is now an end to the chaos, strife and turmoil that had originated in the sea of the past. *See* **Waters**.

SEA OF GLASS – (Rev. 4:6; 15:2) (D&C 77:1; 130:7-9) The earth in its celestial, sanctified, immortal, and eternal state; The *sea of glass* "like unto crystal" imagery is an allusion to the Urim and Thummim.

SEAL[S] – Cover, obstacle or barrier that prevents the contents of something from being revealed to the observer. In the context of Revelation 5:1-5, and chapter 6, the seals are pieces of wax or clay, placed on the edges of a document, which has been wrapped around a stick or rod and then imprinted by a signet or stamp. The wax or clay retains the impression of an emblem or insignia of the owner of the document. The seal serves the following purposes: 1.) Symbolizes authority; 2.) Protects the document; 3.) Identifies the document's owner; 4.) Transfers authority to the appropriate person; 5.) Prevents accidental or inadvertent disclosure of the document; and 6.) Makes the document legally valid. According to tradition each document/page is sealed individually and only the owner or legal administrator may break the seals and open the scroll. It is customary to interpret that after each seal on the scroll in John's vision is broken, a thousand year period of the earth's history comes into view, implying that each seal will reveal the story of our world in one-thousand-year increments after the manner that man measures years (D&C 77:7,13). But some modern scholars and commentators theorize that each seal is symbolic of some significant event. And these defining events do not necessarily fall exactly 1,000 years apart, indicating that the period of time covered by each seal varies and does not represent a period of 1,000 years. However, modern-day revelation and traditional belief suggest that this second interpretation is interesting but incorrect. Though the horsemen and horses, mentioned in association with the breaking of the seals, may not be associated with a particular person or event, they most likely represent an assessment or indication of the mood, most characteristic features, attitude and atmosphere of that specified millennial period in question. The first **four seals** are commonly referred to as the **Four Horsemen of the Apocalypse** (Zech. 1:8-11) because after the seals are broken John describes seeing a separate rider mounted on different colored horses after each seal is broken:

(Rev. 6:1-2) The **first seal** is broken, there is thundering in the heavens and one of the guardian beasts invites John to "come and see" and John sees a **white horse** and a rider with a bow and he went forth "to conquer." This represents the period of time from Adam to Enoch. Since a **white horse** symbolizes victory of the warrior, and **white** is the color of righteousness, we could assume that this rider with a bow and crown is Enoch, a view supported by Moses 7:13-16; 69.

(Rev. 6:3-4) The **second seal** is broken, the second beast says, "Come and see," and John sees a

red horse upon which is mounted a rider with a great **sword** and power to take peace from the earth. The great sword and the color red suggest that this will be an era of war and bloodshed, which it was, and the violence, wickedness and pride was so pervasive during that millennium that the world was destroyed by a flood near the end of the period covered by this seal (Genesis 6:5,11-14; Moses 8:28-29). The phrasing of this verse is remarkably close to one used in modern revelation stating that the time is nigh at hand "when peace shall be taken from the earth, and the devil shall have power over his own dominion" (D&C 1:35). The earth was destroyed by a flood during this period of time. In the last days the earth will be destroyed by fire after a period of time during which evil gathers irreversible momentum over the world.

(Rev. 6:5-6) The **third seal** is broken, and the third beast says, "Come and see," and John sees a **black horse** with the rider holding a pair of **balances** in his hands. A voice announces the onset of a terrible famine. This was the time frame during which some of the most amazing Biblical figures lived, the patriarchs, Abraham, Isaac, Jacob, Joseph, Moses, the Judges. The era ends with the ushering in of the rule of the Israelite kings.

(Rev. 6:8) The **fourth seal** is broken, and the fourth beast says, "Come and see," and John sees a **pale horse** whose rider is named "Death," and "Hell" follows in his wake and "Hell hath enlarged herself, and opened her mouth without measure" (Isaiah 5:14); This is a thousand-year period of unparalleled treachery, terror, violence and oppression on a massive, unprecedented scale, which historically became institutionalized in the form of mighty world empires that rampaged throughout the earth: The Davidic Kingdom collapsed; Israel suffered a civil war from which it never recovered; Cruel and merciless nations such as the Assyrians, Egyptians, Babylonians, Persians, Greeks and Romans enslaved and conquered entire countries; There arose prophets who spent their lives preaching, sorrowing, mourning, some performing mighty miracles and eventually being martyred by apostate kings and traitors (Isaiah 22:1).

(Rev. 6: 9-11) The **fifth seal** is opened and John sees the souls of those who have been killed and who have perished for their testimonies of Jesus Christ under the altar of God. They petition God for justice to be exercised upon the earth but they are admonished to "rest for a season." Traditional belief maintains that the birth of Christ marks the end of the fourth seal and the opening of the fifth seal. However, modern scholars hold to the popular idea that the mortal Messiah lived during the fourth seal and his resurrection marks the opening of the fifth seal; two interesting interpretations, but modern revelation has not addressed this yet.

(Rev. 6:12-17) The **sixth seal** is opened and John observes scenes of great confusion, devastation and destruction; these events are obviously the distinguishing occurrences that mark the end of the sixth thousand years and the beginning of the seventh, and represent the judgements of God upon the world. The Restoration of the gospel is accomplished during the period of time covered by the sixth seal (Isaiah 29:6; D&C 77:9-10).

(Rev. 8:1-5) The **seventh seal** is opened and there is silence in heaven for a space of half an hour; the silence in heaven may be indicative of the sorrow in heaven over the state of the fallen world, and a short time for heavenly reflection on the solemn task ahead—the reaping down and harvesting of the wicked that rejected the Messiah, who will soon be cast into hell as a final and definitive answer to the prayers of the saints, past and present, who pray for the world to be saved and that they might be delivered from Babylon. The prayers are represented by the rising incense. Fire is taken from the altar, placed in a censer and cast upon the earth after the half hour of silence. The altar of God is usually associated with worship, peace, safety and sanctuary, but now the altar is the place from which the cleansing of the world begins, signifying that the time for repentance is nearly over; There are thunderings, earthquakes and lightning as never seen before in the history of the world. These events are followed by the sounding of the trumpets and the pouring of God's punishments from the vials of the altar. [It is important to note that the seventh seal, or the final Millennium does not begin with the Second Coming of Christ in glory.]

SEAL/NAME OF GOD IN THE FOREHEAD – (Rev. 7:3; 9:4; 22:4) (Ezek. 9:4-6; D&C 77:9; 109:38; 132:19-20) Blessed by the ordinances and covenants of the priesthood. One of the benefits to be derived from bearing this "seal" is to be afforded the protection and guidance of Him whose seal it is. This is significant considering the horrific impending judgments about to be unleashed upon the world; The sealing power as that of Elijah; (Rev. 14:1) This **seal** may be a synonym for the "Father's name written in their foreheads." This phrase reflects the practice of some peoples who mark their foreheads with a sign or symbol representing the object of their faith or the god they worship.

SEASON – (Rev. 6:11; 20:3) (D&C 43:31) Period of time that is unspecified to man, but the purpose and length of which is measured unto God.

SEARCHES THE REINS – (Rev. 2:23) God examines the understanding of every mortal. In His omniscience He perceives everything.

SEAT – (Rev. 2:13) Earthly position from whence Satan assumes his pretentious authority and reigns over the world. Compare with God's throne, from whence God rules over the universe. **Seat** connotes a temporary position of power while **throne** denotes permanence.

SECOND COMING OF JESUS CHRIST, FINAL FALL OF SATAN AND DESTRUCTION OF BABYLON – (Rev. 6:12-17; 11:19; 14:8-11; 19:1-9, 11-13) Any remaining vestiges of Babylon and her minions, which survived the tribulations, will be utterly destroyed once and for all, both physically and spiritually, at the Second Coming of Christ. The glory of the returning King and his saints will be so brilliant and radiant that Satan and darkness will flee and be confined to the abyss, having been driven there by the righteousness and goodness of the Lord and the resurrected saints. Michael, the mighty angel, will take the keys of hell and shut the cell door against the devil. The angel locks the dragon away with the key to the gates of hell. Satan is bound with chains and then the pit is sealed.

SECOND COMING/ REDEMPTION OF SAINTS/ APPEARANCE OF CHRIST IN GLORY AND POWER – (Rev. 1:7; 19:11-16; 21:3-7) (Isaiah 40:5; 52:10; 66:18; Jude 1:14-15; D&C 34:6; 45:47-53) The King's millennial reign is described by the Seer as beginning thus: "Behold, the tabernacle of God is with men, and he will dwell with them, . . . and be their God," and the Christ will say, "He that **over-cometh** shall inherit all things; and I will be his God, and he shall be my son."

SECOND DEATH – (Rev. 2:11; 20:6,14-15; 21:8) (Jacob 3:11; D&C 29:27-28; 63:17) Spiritual death, separation from God; Exclusion from the **New Jerusalem**.

SEED – (Rev. 12:17) Children, descendants; Followers, adherents.

SELFISHNESS – *See* **Materialism**.

SERPENT – (Rev. 9:19; 12:9,14-15; 20:2) (Gen. 3:1,13-14; Moses 4:5-10; 19-20) Satanic; Satan, the devil; Synonym for **Dragon**.

SEVEN [7]—Number symbolic of totality, perfection, completeness:

Seven golden candlesticks are the seven churches of Asia (Rev. 1:4,11,20) that John wrote to but represent all the congregations of the saints.

Seven Beatitudes and Seven attributes of God. (Rev. 5:12; 7:12) *See* **Blessings for the Righteous**.

Seven angels who sound trumpets and pour God's judgments upon the earth (Rev. 8:2; 15:1).

Seven heads of the beast (Rev. 13:1); the seven

heads, seven mountains/hills [Rome], and seven kings with one crown each may be specific leaders of earthly kingdoms or nations in the latter-days unto which Satan gives much power and cunning. They symbolize the power and evil that upholds and sustains Babylon.

Seven horns of the Lamb—Corrected by Joseph Smith to twelve horns representing the Twelve Apostles (Rev. 5:6).

Seven lamps before the throne of God, which are the seven spirits [servants] (Rev. 4:5).

Seven mountains—Possibly an allusion to Rome (Rev. 17:9).

Seven kings—Represent the kingdoms, power and corruption of Babylon and her abominations. The seven kings may refer to specific powerful rulers in the last days that exercise dominion over the world (Rev. 17:10).

Seven seals—(Rev. 1:20) Each of the seals on the scroll covers a 1,000 year portion of the Book of the Lamb, or history of the world.

Seven spirits/ fiery lamps/ angels of the churches/(Rev. 1:7,20; 4:5; 5:6) eyes of the Lamb—Represent or are symbolic of mortal priesthood servants who magnify their callings; Apostles and prophets.

Seven thunders—Not interpreted (Rev. 10:3-4).

Seven trumpets announce the judgments of God (Rev. 8:2-11:18).

Seven plagues afflict the world (Rev. 15:1,6; 16:1-21) (Lev. 26:21).

Seven vials full of the wrath of God (Rev. 15:7).

Seven stars—(Rev. 1:16; 3:1). The seven servants

[rendered angels in KJV of Bible] of the seven churches [seven candlesticks which by extension represent all the servants of all the congregations of the saints.

SHIVERS – (Rev. 2:27) Fragments, pieces.

SHORTLY – (Rev. 1:1) As in the phrase "*shortly come to pass*," it means at some date yet in the future. *See* **Quickly.**

SICKLE – (Rev. 14:14) Tool or implement used to cut down and harvest a crop, as wheat for example; The image of the harvest often is used to represent the people of the earth who are ready to receive the gospel (Matt. 9:37-38; Mark 4:29; Alma 17:13; 26:5-7); The sickle is also a symbol of judgment and death (Rev. 14:19) (Joel 3:12-13).

SIGN IN HEAVEN – (Rev. 15:1) *See* **Wonder**

SIGNS OF THE LAST DAYS – *See* **Last Days**, **Tribulation, Curses**; Note that **signs** is a term sometimes synonymous with **miracles, wonders**, etc. Throughout the scriptures, believers are warned as to what the signs of the **Second Coming** and end of the world will be through the use of multiple fulfillments of prophecy and the establishing of shadows, types and patterns. For in the **last days** we will observe conduct and behaviors in peoples that characterized our predecessors during the time of Noah, the Jews during the time of Christ, and the most compelling of all, the ancient Nephite and Lamanite societies at the time of the Lord's crucifixion and resurrection. (Rev. 17-19) (D&C 45:22-44; 88:87-95; JS-Matthew 1:23-37) One of the clearest warnings regarding the **signs of the last days** is found in the Book of Mormon:

"Then shall my revelations which I have caused to be written by my servant John be unfolded in the eyes of all people. Remember, when ye see these things, ye shall know that the time is at hand that they shall be made manifest in very deed" (Ether 4:15-16).

SIGNIFIED IT – (Rev. 1:1) Showed it, revealed it.

SILENCE IN HEAVEN FOR HALF AN HOUR – (Rev. 8:1) (D&C 88:95) The **silence in heaven**, which marks the breaking of the seventh seal, has been interpreted in many different ways. Some explanations for the "silence" may be: 1.) There will be an absence of communication between earthly and heavenly beings; 2.) There will be literal calm and quiet in the physical realms of the earth and firmament; 3.) The silence of heavenly hosts will be brought about due to anticipation or expectation of what is about to happen upon the face of the earth (Zeph. 1:7); 4.) The powers of darkness and evil will be so powerful upon the earth that it causes "silence to reign, and all eternity is pained" (D&C 38:11-12); 5.) Silence that is similar to or characteristic of the calm before a storm for God is about to release His punishing judgments upon the earth. (Psalms 50:3-4; 35:22-23; 83:1-2; Isaiah 65:6). The phrase **half an hour** is to be interpreted as being either symbolic or as a relatively short period of time, possibly 21 years according to the Lord's reckoning of time (2 Peter 3:8).

SILK – (Rev. 18:12) (Ezek. 16:10,13) One of the treasured, fine and rare items of cloth in which the merchants of Babylon trafficked. Silk is associated with wealth, power and royalty.

SIN – Sin will be rampant in the last days just prior to the punishing judgments that await unrepentant sinners (Rev. 9:20-21; 21:8; 21:27) and it is beyond the scope of this study aid to enumerate the multitude of sins of our era, but it suffices to say that John focuses on the most pertinent and dangerous sins of the last days that will eventually bring to pass the end of the world: apostasy, idolatry, selfishness, materialism, fear, violence and corruption.

SION – *See* **Mount Sion/Zion**.

SIT/SITTETH – (Rev. 3:21; 4:4; 5:13; 6:16; 7:10,15) God, His Son and the redeemed of God sit upon a throne in heaven. (17:1,3,9,15; 18:7) Contrast the glory of God's throne with the Queen Babylon that sits upon the restlessness and instability of the **waters**, the **beast**, the **seven mountains** and the peoples of the earth.

SIX [6] – If seven is symbolic of totality or perfection, six may be symbolic of having fallen short of perfection; incomplete.

SIX HUNDRED THREE SCORE AND SIX [666] – The numeric representation of the name of the second beast, or anti-Christ. The name, 666, may correspond to an actual name or it may be strictly symbolic in its application.

SMOKE – (Rev. 15:8) *See* **Cloud**. The source of the **smoke** is the "glory of God" and "his power."

SMOKE FROM THE PIT – (Rev. 9:2-3) (Moses 4:4; 7:26; 1 Nephi 8:23) Darkness that ascends from the **pit**, or hell, and engulfs the entire earth. The imagery of smoke is used to indicate Satan's ability to blind and deceive man.

SMOKE OF INCENSE – (Rev. 8:3-4) Prayers of the saints.

SMOKE OF THEIR TORMENT – (Rev. 14:11) (Isaiah 34:8-10) Symbolic of the eternal nature of God's punishment of the wicked following their destruction by **fire and brimstone**. (Rev. 17:16; 18:9,18; 19:3) Babylon will be destroyed by fire and smoke will ascend "for ever and ever" as a reminder of her sinful nature and fallen condition. Contrast these images with that of the sweet burning of incense that represents the prayers of the righteous.

SMYRNA – (Rev. 2:8-11) A prosperous commercial center in Asia Minor, and is now a large city in present day Turkey named Izmir; The saints of Smyrna were a group of poor, weak, humble believers who were severely persecuted by the local Jewish population. The Lord, through John, urges them to "fear not" the things that they are suffering in the flesh, for the Lord has power to deliver them from the "second death" and give them a crown of eternal life. The congregations at Philadelphia and at Smyrna were the only groups NOT to receive a rebuke from the Lord.

SODOM – (Rev. 11:8) (Isaiah 1:10; 3:9; 2 Peter 2:6) **Sodom** and **Egypt** are used as metaphors or symbols for a wicked and apostate Jerusalem of the latter days.

SON OF MAN – (Rev. 1:13; 14:14) (Dan. 7:13; Moses 6:57; Abr. 3:27) Jesus Christ.

SONG, NEW – (Rev. 14:3) (Isaiah 42:9-10; D&C 84:96-102) Song of redemption to be sung by those who have "overcome."

SONG OF MOSES – (Rev. 15:3) Song of deliverance; Song of salvation.

SONG OF THE LAMB – (Rev. 15:3) (D&C 133:56) Song of salvation and praise.

SORCERIES – (Rev. 9:21; 18:23) (Isaiah 47:9; Mormon 1:19) Witchcraft, divinations, necromancy, enchantments, fascination with the occult; Illicit drug use. Through sorcery its practitioners attempt to invoke unseen powers in attempts to imitate the power of God and gain believers.

SPIRIT OF REVELATION/ TESTIMONY/ PROPHECY – (Rev. 1:2, 11; 2:7; 3:22; 11:7; 12:7,11,17; 19:10; 20:4; 22:10) (Alma 17:2-3; D&C 18:34) The Spirit of Revelation is to be interpreted as having a testimony that Jesus is the Christ, the Son of God, and prophecy is to be interpreted as making that testimony known to others. The writings of John in the book of Revelation are prophetic, therefore, they are a testimony and easy to be understood by those with the gift and spirit of revelation; *See* **Understanding**. John informs the readers that those who keep the words of this book will also be shown "the things which must shortly be done" (Rev. 22:6-7). President Brigham Young desired that all men would be prophets and filled with the gift of revelation (**CR**, April 6 1853). Moses mourned greatly over the smallness, bickering and complaining of the children of Israel. In Numbers chapter 11 we read that God begins to destroy the people by fire for their sins of ingratitude and murmuring. Moses was instructed to not bear the burden of leadership alone, but to choose seventy elders from among the people to assist him. God

118

spoke to them, they were filled with the Spirit and they "prophesied and did not cease." To Joshua, the servant of Moses, this appeared unseemly and he complained to Moses, and Moses replied, "Enviest thou? Would God that all the Lord's people were prophets" (Numbers 11:28-29). Regarding personal revelation the Prophet Joseph remarked, "A person may profit by noticing the first intimation of the spirit of revelation. When you feel pure intelligence flowing unto you—it may give you sudden strokes of ideas" (**TPJS**, p. 151).

SPIRIT, IN THE – (Rev. 1:10; 4:2; 17:3; 21:10) Transfigured or transformed temporarily to a higher level of spirituality in order to withstand the presence of deity, "quickened by the Spirit;" To be conveyed or transported by the Spirit to another location (Ezek. 3:14; 37:1; 43:5; Dan. 10:7-10; 1 Cor. 13:12; 2 Cor. 12:2-4; 1 Nephi 1:8; D&C 76:11; Moses 6:64).

SPUE/SPEW – (Rev. 3:16) To vomit, regurgitate. Figuratively speaking, the Lord will reject those that are "lukewarm" and spew them, as it were, "out of His mouth."

STAND – (Rev. 6:17; 10:5; 15:2) (Psalms 76:7; 130:3; Mal. 3:2; D&C 29:11) *See* **Feet**.

STAR[S] – Individual human beings, personalities; Children of our Father in Heaven (Rev. 1:16,20; 12:4) (Gen. 37:9; Job 38:7; Dan. 8:10).

STAR, BRIGHT AND MORNING – Jesus Christ (Rev. 2:28; 22:16) (2 Peter 1:19)

STAR CALLED WORMWOOD – (Rev. 8:11) Since **wormwood** is a symbol for bitterness, the **star 'wormwood'** may be representative of a person who causes great bitterness or an angel [the devil] which is destined to bring a very bitter scourge upon the earth. It is unlikely that **wormwood** corresponds to *natural* disasters since **star** is a representation of a person [or spirit being], so it is logical to consider that **wormwood** could refer to *man-made* disasters or catastrophes of gigantic scale or proportion which serve as a source of great bitterness, sorrow and mourning.

STAR FALLEN FROM HEAVEN – Lucifer (Rev. 8:10; 9:1; 12:7-9) (Isaiah 14:12; Luke 10:18); *See* **Star called Wormwood**.

STARS FELL UNTO THE EARTH – (Rev. 6:13) (Isaiah 13:10; Joel 2:10; 3:15; Matt. 24:29; D&C 29:14: 34:9; 45:42; 88:87) In the same way that the sun will refuse to give its light and the moon will turn to blood, the day will come that due to some cataclysmic event, the stars of the heavens will appear to fall and refuse to shine; John may have seen other things that he interpreted as being stars literally falling from the skies, things such as missiles, jets, satellites or meteors.

STARS, SEVEN – (Rev. 1:16,20) The seven servants or leaders of the seven churches in Asia.

STARS, TWELVE – (Rev. 12:1) Completeness of priesthood power such as the Apostleship; Twelve tribes of Israel.

STINGS IN THEIR TAILS – (Rev. 9:10) *See* **Scorpions**.

STONE, WHITE — *See* **White Stone**.

STONES, PRECIOUS – *See* **Precious Stones**.

STREET – (Rev. 21:21; 22:2) The New Jerusalem is noted as having a street. It's not clear why a more generic word such as path, way, route wasn't used unless it's to make the New Jerusalem appear larger and more urban and less abstract to the reader.

SUFFER — (Rev. 11:9) Permit, allow.

SUN – (Rev. 16:8-9) Symbol for a source of torment, turmoil, or punishment from God because of its unrelenting heat; (Rev. 7:16) (Psalms 121:6; Isaiah 49:10) The sun will not be able to "smite" the righteous because of the mercies of the Lord; (Rev. 1:16; 10:1) The Lord's countenance, as that of His celestial messengers, is "as the sun in his strength" (Mal. 4:2; Matt. 17:2; D&C 110:3).

SUN BECOMES BLACK/DARKENED – (Rev. 6:12) (Isaiah 13:10; Jeremiah 4:28; Joel 2:31; 3:15; Matt. 24:29; Acts 2:20; D&C 29:14; 34:9; 45:42; 88:87; 133:49) The image of the sun turning black as with sackcloth indicates that the heavens will be in mourning over the wickedness found upon the earth; It is possible that in the last days, the sun will be darkened by smoke from man-made or natural fires, volcanic eruptions or some unexplained astronomical event.

SUN, CLOTHED WITH THE – (Rev. 12:1) Encompassed about by the glory of the sun.

SUPPER OF THE GREAT GOD – (Rev. 19:17-18,21) (Isaiah 18:6; Ezek. 39:4,8-22; D&C 29:18,20) Following the war and tribulation lasting 42 months, Israel will burn materials from the destroyed army for **seven** years. The fowls of the air, flies and beasts of the field will participate in the "**supper of the great God**" and devour the carcasses of those slain in battle.

SWORD – (Rev. 19:11-21) John recorded in the book

of Revelation that the Lord will return to the earth with a sharp sword to "smite the nations" when he comes to judge the world; Symbol of impending destruction (Ezek. 21:3; Mormon 8:41; D&C 1:13; 35:14; 45:33); The **sword** may also serve as a symbol or metaphor for a person or agent that will perform the Lord's work that may or may not necessarily be a work of destruction (Rev. 2:16).

SWORD, TWO-EDGED/DOUBLE-EDGED – Truth, Word of God (Rev. 1:16; 2:12) (Psalms 149:6; Heb. 4:12; D&C 6:2; 33:1).

SYMBOLISM, Its purpose and John's literary use of – John employs symbols and symbolism throughout the book of Revelation for the purpose of protecting the message [and messenger] and for the edification and enlightenment of the spiritually endowed. Since the natural languages of man are fraught with ambiguities, confusion and are vulnerable to misinterpretation and corruption, the skillful use of symbols conveys complex and extensive ideas and concepts with the minimal use of words. Behind every symbol stands an array of temporal and spiritual realities that are easily discernible to the human mind. Elder John Widtsoe [Latter-day Apostle 1921-1952] wrote: "We know things only so far as our senses permit. Whatever is known, is known through symbols. The letters on the written page are but symbols. Man lives under a great system of symbolism. Clearly, the mighty, eternal truths encompassing all that man is or may be, cannot be expressed literally . . . By the use of symbols of speech, of action, of color, of form, the great truths connected with the story of man are made evident to the mind" (*Rational Theology*, p. 120).

SYNAGOGUE OF SATAN – (Rev. 2:9; 3:9) The Jewish congregations in Smyrna who persecuted the saints and rejected the gospel of Christ.

_◯_

TABERNACLE – Tent (Isaiah 4:6; D&C 124:38); Mortal body; presence or personage/countenance of a being (Rev. 7:15; 15:5; 21:3) (Lev. 26:11-12; Zech. 14:16).

TABERNACLE OF THE TESTIMONY – (Rev. 15:5) Also known as the Tabernacle of witness. (Num. 17:7) Tabernacle of Moses that served as a temple for the children of Israel until the erection of Solomon's Temple. The **testimony** refers to the two tablets upon which the law of God was written.

TALENT – (Rev. 16:21) Ancient measure of weight that is equivalent to about 60-80 pounds. Hail stones with a weight of a **talent** will be one of God's final demonstrations of His wrath against the wicked inhabitants of the world.

TEARS – (Rev. 7:17; 21:4) Throughout Biblical *and* human history a variety of circumstances may give rise to the shedding of tears: mourning, grief, oppression, physical pain, humility and compassion; but regardless of the reason for the tears, relief will come for the redeemed as "God shall wipe away all tears from the eyes."

TEETH — (Rev. 9:8) (Joel 1:6) Symbol of destructive power.

TEMPLE, NO MAN WAS ABLE TO ENTER –
(Rev. 15:8) The time for man to pray and plead for
forgiveness has passed. The plagues reserved for the
wicked and unrepentant will follow their decreed
course until complete. Only after the plagues will
the people who remain approach God for mercy.

TEMPLE OF HEAVEN/IN HEAVEN – Celestial
kingdom (Rev. 3:12; 4:1; 7:15; 11:19; 14:17; 16:17)
where God's throne exists; Upon being redeemed
and sanctified, the **New Jerusalem** will not have a
temple "for the Lord God Almighty and the Lamb
are the temple of it" (Rev. 21:22).

TEN [10]/TENTH – (Rev. 2:10; 11:13; 17:12-13)
(Num. 14:22; Job 19:3; Dan. 1:12,14,20; Neh. 4:12)
Number symbolic of law [the Ten Commandments],
but not the complete gospel; Number associated
with temptation and trial; Completeness in terms of
being a subset of a greater whole; Totality in the
physical, mortal sense, but not in the eternal sense;
Compare with the number twelve, which is
symbolic of wholeness and completeness in terms
of authority and priesthood; Ten and multiples of
ten are representative of magnitude of number or
abundance of something.

TEN DAYS – (Rev. 2:10) The saints will suffer trials
and tribulation for a significant amount of time,
however that time is short compared with the
eternal life that awaits them if they endure well.

**TEN THOUSAND TIMES TEN THOUSAND AND
THOUSANDS OF THOUSANDS** – (Rev. 5:11)
Number of infinite magnitude.

TESTIMONY – *See* **Spirit of Revelation**. (Rev. 1:2;
12:11,17; 19:10) (Ps. 19:7; Acts 14:3; 1 Cor. 1:6; 2:1;

12:3; 2 Cor. 1:12; Gal. 1:12; 2 Tim. 1:8; D&C 58:6; 62:3; 76:22,50,74,79; 84:62,81,88; 88:88-90; 100:10; 124:20; 136:39; 138:12; Moses 7:27,62; JS-H 1:26; Alma 4:20; 6:8; 7:13); (Rev. 1:9) John is exiled to Patmos "for the word of God, and for the **testimony** of Jesus Christ;" Martyrs were slain for their **testimony** of Jesus Christ. (Rev. 6:9; 11:7) (D&C 135:7) *See* **Word of God**. (Rev. 15:5)

THIEF – (Rev. 3:3; 16:15) (1 Thess. 5:2,4; 2 Peter 3:10; D&C 45:19; 106:4-5) The Lord's return, or the Day of the Lord as it is called elsewhere, is described as the intrusion of a "thief" who comes when one is unprepared and unsuspecting. *See* **Quickly**.

THIRD PART – (Rev. 8:11-12, 9:18) Fractional part or portion of a whole; (Rev. 12:4) (D&C 29:36) That part or percentage of pre-mortal spirits who did not keep their first estate and were cast out of heaven with Lucifer.

THOUSAND[S] – (Jude 1:14) Number signifying a great magnitude. Multiples of 1,000 represent great multitudes and not necessarily the precise number recorded.

THOUSAND TWO HUNDRED AND THREE-SCORE [1,260] DAYS – (Rev. 11:3) The length of time that the **two witnesses** minister to the people of Jerusalem. *See* **Three and a Half**.

THOUSAND TWO HUNDRED AND THREE-SCORE [1,260] YEARS – (Rev. 12:6) The length of time that the Church is sheltered "in the wilderness" and that mortals languish on earth in a state of apostasy. *See* **Three and a Half**.

THOUSAND YEARS – *See* entries for **Millennium** and **Seals**.

THREE [3] – Number symbolic of completeness which is formed by individual parts. The holy trinity is composed of three personages. A presidency/bishopric consists of three persons. The world is composed of three parts—heaven, earth and the seas and/or that which is under the earth [or more precisely, heaven, earth, and non-earth or firmament]; Jesus' body was in the tomb for three days; Three 6's represent the beast's identity, name, or the mark of the beast—which could also be a trinity of sorts—the dragon, the beast, and the anti-Christ. There is the tradition that "666" is the numeric rendition of the name of the anti-Christ/Beast.

THREE AND A HALF – (Rev. 11:2-3; 12:6; 13:5) Half of seven; Number that has a negative connotation because it implies a disruption or lack of continuity. The Gentiles lay siege to and plunder Jerusalem for 42 months [**three and a half** years]. (Rev. 11:9,11) The two witnesses/prophets lie in the streets of Jerusalem while the Gentiles celebrate their deaths for **three and a half** days. (Dan. 7:25) The beast speaks blasphemy against God for 42 months. If we interpret **three and a half** in Old Testament context we know that Israel was struck with a famine for **three and a half** years during the time of the prophet Elijah. (Luke 4:25; James 5:17) From this experience we may reason that **three and a half** days/months/years represent a time of famine, darkness and apostasy.

THREE PARTS, CITY WAS DIVIDED INTO – (Rev. 16:19) The great city, probably Babylon, is now weakened and prepared for destruction.

THRONE[S] – (Rev. 1:4; 4:2-3,9; 5:1,7,13; 6:16; 7:9-11,15; 12:5; 14:3,5; 16:17; 19:4; 20:4; 21:5; 22:1,3) (Psalms 47:8; Isaiah 6:1; Ezek. 1:26) God sits upon a royal chair or "great white **throne**" in heaven, from which He issues His divine decrees, and from which He will judge the world. (Rev. 20:11) The heavenly throne is symbolic of God's power, dominion and universal sovereignty; Faithful Saints who "overcome" will be privileged to sit with the Father on His throne which means they "are not angels, but are gods." (Rev. 3:21) (D&C 132:37; Moses 7:59); Satan, the anti-Christ and the beast have a throne on the earth, but it is called a "seat," (Rev. 2:13; 13:2; 16:10) indicating that Satan's power is temporary. It is confined and fixed in terms of time and dominion.

THUNDER/THUNDERINGS – (Rev. 6:1; 10:3; 14:2; 19:6) (D&C 43:21; 133:22) Indicative of God's power or strength. Used in such phrases as "voice of thunder," it represents a force that transcends nature and invokes awe and attention.

THYATIRA – (Rev. 2:18-29) City in Asia Minor, affluent community of traders, merchants and craftsmen; The Lord condemns the activities of one **Jezebel**, a false prophetess, that seduced the Lord's servants to commit fornication and engage in idolatrous practices. The Lord also admonished those who were true to the faith to stay the course. If they do so, their testimonies will be strengthened.

THYINE WOOD – (Rev. 18:12) Also known as Citron, a tree of the cypress family that is native to the northwest coast of Africa. The fragrance and deep reddish-brown color of this wood made it very popular and extremely valuable. It was reportedly worth its weight in gold.

TIME – As in the phrases "**Time** is at hand" (Rev. 1:3; 22:10), "**Time** is short" (Rev. 12:12), "There should be **time** no longer" (Rev. 10:6) (D&C 88:110); Our existence in mortality is measured by **time**. It is but a probationary period. It is Satan's only chance to exact revenge and tempt and torment the children of our Heavenly Father. Time in the mortal world according to man's reckoning is a concept interpreted as a constant—unchanging and unyielding; To John the Revelator, the prophets and to God, there is no **time**. Furthermore, this concept of time carries with it the idea that there shall be no more delay. The time allotted for repenting and reforming is growing shorter and shorter (Alma 40:8; D&C 84:100; 88:110).

TIME, AND TIMES, AND HALF A TIME – (Rev. 12:14) (Dan. 12:7) Interpreted as being the number **Three and a Half**.

TOPAZ – (Rev. 21:20) Precious stone, yellow and green in color, included in the foundation of the wall of the **New Jerusalem**; Found on the breastplate of the high priest (Ex. 28:17; 39:10).

TONGUE — (Rev. 16:10) (D&C 29:19) Organ of the body associated with the ability to speak and express one's thoughts and desires. To lose the use of one's tongue is to be denied power and influence.

TRAVAILING – (Rev. 12:2) To be in labor.

TREE[S] – (Rev. 7:1,3; 11:4) (Psalms 1:3; Isaiah 10:17-19; Ezek. 31:14; Dan. 4:10,17; Zech. 11:1-2) Throughout the Old Testament trees in their many varieties have been used to symbolize persons or peoples.

TREE OF LIFE – "Love of God" as embodied in Jesus Christ. (Rev. 2:7; 22:2,14) (Jeremiah 17:7-8; John 3:16; 1 Nephi 8:10-12; 11:25; Alma 5:34) The **Tree of Life** bears "**twelve**" types of fruit each month all year round.

TRIBES OF THE CHILDREN OF ISRAEL – (Rev. 7:4) The redeemed and chosen High Priests who are to serve the Father and "follow the Lamb" are to be selected from all the tribes of Israel. John records them as being in this order: Judah, Reuben, Gad, Asher, Nepthalim, Manasseh, Simeon, Levi, Issachar, Zabulon, Joseph and Benjamin. For some unknown reason the tribe of Dan and that of the other son of Joseph, Ephraim, are not included in this list.

TRIBULATION – (Rev. 2:10,22; 7:13-14) (John 16:13; 2 Tim. 3:12; D&C 58:2-4; 78:14; 138:13) [Note the use in singular.] Refining affliction that one must pass through before receiving a Celestial inheritance. God permits his servants in the performance of their missions in mortality to suffer and most often the Lord does not remove the source of personal affliction. John introduces himself in the book of Revelation as " . . . your brother, and companion in **tribulation**" (Rev. 1:9). The Prophet Joseph Smith begins his notable doctrinal letter of January 1834 to the Elders in Missouri: "Brethren in Christ, and Companions in **Tribulation**" (**HC**, Vol. 2, page 4). Tribulation is meant to prompt one to repentance.

TRIBULATIONS/CALAMITIES/AFFLIC-

TIONS/PLAGUES [OF THE LAST DAYS] –
The tribulations of the last days include but are not
limited to: war [and all manner of violence], sin and
temptation [including all types of corruption and
perversion], affliction, hardship, adversity, famine,
plagues, earthquakes, floods, thunder, lightning,
wind, drought, hail, fire, wonders in the heavens,
etc.; These **tribulations** are sometimes referred to
by Biblical scholars as "Covenant Curses" in that
they come after prophetic warnings and after God's
children have had the chance to accept Christ, the
priesthood and the covenant blessings associated
with the priesthood (Rev. 6:12-13; 8:7-9; 11:13;
16:17-20) (Brigham Young, **JD** 8:123; D&C 43:23-
26; 45:33,40-42; 88:88-89; Moses 7:61). *See*
Persecution.

TRUMPET – (Rev. 1:10; 4:1) (D&C 77:12; 88:92-110)
The Lord's voice is compared to the sound of a
trumpet; (Isaiah 27:13; Joel 2:1; Zeph. 1:14; Zech.
9:14; D&C 29:13) The sounding of the trumpet will
be used to announce the "Day of the Lord," or in
other words, the Day of Judgment. The trumpet is
an instrument used to sound forthcoming
announcements or judgments. In the book of
Revelation there are seven angels that blow the
seven trumpets to summon judgments, plagues
and woes upon the wicked, affording them an
opportunity to repent even during the last moments
of the existence of the mortal world as we know it
(D&C 29:17: " . . . behold, my blood will not cleanse
them if they hear me not."); The warning of the
seven trumpets harks back to a warning contained
in Leviticus 26:18,21,28: "I will punish you seven

times more for your sins . . . I will bring seven times more plagues upon you according to your sins . . . I, even I will chastise you seven times for your sins." The sounding of these trumpets will take place at the beginning of the opening of the **seventh seal** (D&C 77:12) after silence "for a space of half an hour."

(Rev. 8:7) Hail, fire and blood will shower upon the earth [reference to a 'Sodom and Gomorrah'-type destruction].

(Rev. 8:8-9) Great burning consumes the sea and a third part of all things in and on the sea perish. (Jeremiah 51:25; Ezekiel 10:2-7)

(Rev. 8:10-11) A burning star falls upon the waters, rivers, and fountains of waters and poisons the water [reference to **wormwood** and the waters being bitter and toxic, causing death].

(Rev. 8:12) The sun, moon and stars are darkened (Ex. 10:21; Isaiah 13:10; Joel 2:1-2; Amos 5:18,20).

(Rev. 9:1-12) The "bottomless pit" is opened, and "smoke" and "locusts" are released for five months upon the world. (Ex. 10:15) [At the sounding of the fifth trumpet, the first 'woe' is in progress].

(Rev. 9:13-21) The second 'woe' begins at the sixth trumpet blast, and great armies assemble on the face of the earth and the 'four destroying angels' begin their work of destruction.

(Rev 11:15-19) The third 'woe' starts when the seventh trumpet sounds, and it announces the destruction of the earth's political kingdoms and the onset of the glory and reign of God upon the earth; The heavens are opened and the earth is enveloped in blinding lightning, thunder, fire and hail, and the few wicked that survive to blaspheme God are destroyed by servants/angels of God.

TRUTH/LIGHT – (Rev. 1:12,20) (3 Nephi 18:24) The true Church of Christ is to safeguard and teach the **Truth**, or in other words, teach the saving doctrines and ordinances of Jesus Christ. **Light** is often used in combination with or as a synonym for the divine truths of the gospel, that is, the knowledge of the **Truth** that comes from the ultimate source of **Truth**, Jesus Christ. This knowledge comes by way of personal visitation, the Holy Ghost, dreams, the Lord's servants [scripture and public discourses], or revelations and visions. In the context of deliverance/salvation it is vital that the Saints learn the **Truth** and the doctrine of Jesus Christ in order to distinguish between Light and Darkness, Truth and Error, Freedom and Captivity (2 Cor. 3:17; D&C123:12,17); We often use the expression "Light of Christ" to refer to man's intuition and innate desire to believe in God and recognize that man is literally the spiritual offspring of God. The word "conscience" is associated with the term "Light of Christ." In the context of the **New Jerusalem**, the Holy City will have no need of the sun or other source of light "for the glory of God did lighten it, and the Lamb is the light thereof. "There shall be no night there" (Rev. 21:23,25).

TWELVE [**12**] – Number symbolic of wholeness, completeness as pertaining to the authority, power, and priesthood/tribes of Israel. Present day priesthood quorums are organized and numbered in multiples of twelve.

TWELVE APOSTLES/PROPHETS – (Rev. 21:14)

The names of the twelve Apostles are inscribed upon the foundations of the **New Jerusalem**; Apostles are special witnesses of Jesus Christ who are to teach the gospel to the inhabitants of all nations of the world (Matt. 28:16–19; Mark 16:14–15; Luke 24:47–48; John 21:15–17; Mosiah 3:13; Alma 29:8; D&C 42:58; D&C 107:33; D&C 134:12).

TWELVE GATES to the New Jerusalem/ Heavenly City – (Rev. 21:12-13) There are three gates on each of the four walls of the New Jerusalem. Above the gates are inscribed the names of the twelve tribes of Israel and the gates are watched over by twelve angels.

TWENTY FOUR [24] ELDERS – (Rev. 5:8,14) *See* **Elders, Four and Twenty**.

TWO [2]– Number associated with witnesses and the establishment of truth; Number that implies division, separation, opposites.

TWO-EDGED SWORD — *See* Sword, two edged.

TWO HUNDRED THOUSAND THOUSAND – (Rev. 9:16) Two hundred million; An innumerable host; Multitude of armies.

TWO WITNESSES — See **Witnesses**.

-𝒰-

UNCLEAN — (Rev. 16:3; 18:2) Impure, abominable, demonic.

UNDERSTANDING – (Rev. 13:18) (Mosiah 2:9; D&C 136:32; Job 32:8; Zech. 7:11; Jeremiah 3:15; Ezek. 12:2) Understanding is that special event where one's perception and experience, knowledge, action, and attitude all intersect. The true understanding of John's vision [or of any inspired revelation] is awakened in us. Our minds become enlightened to the degree that we follow John's instructions to read, hear and keep the words of the revelation (Rev. 1:2). It is an active process that requires searching, pondering, praying, the faithful exercising of our stewardships and a continual remembrance that the Lord will be faithful in his promises. In regard to understanding the scriptures, the Prophet Joseph wrote: "He who reads it oftenest will like it best, and he who is acquainted with it, will know [recognize] the hand [of the Lord] wherever he can see it" (**History of the Church, Volume 2**, page 14).

UNTIMELY FIGS – (Rev. 6:13) *See* **Fig Tree**.

URIM AND THUMMIM – (Rev. 15:2) (D&C 130:8) God's residence is described as being a "great Urim and Thummim. John the Revelator described such a place as being "a sea of glass mingled with fire."

$$- \mathcal{O} \mathcal{V} -$$

VESSELS – (Rev. 2:27) (Psalms 31:12; Acts 9:15; 1 Thess. 4:4; 2 Tim. 2:21; 1 Peter 3:7; D&C 76:33) Containers, receptacles. Metaphor for the mortal body or person.

VESTURE – (Rev. 19:13,16) Clothing, apparel, outer garment, robe.

VIALS/BOWLS/CENSERS – (Rev. 15:7) In chapter 16 of the book of Revelation John repeats a scenario of angels cursing the earth using slightly different symbolism and imagery than that of the trumpets and plagues spoken of in chapters 8 to 11. Why? Some commentators think that this is a vision of a second round of plagues and afflictions that will finish the cleansing of the earth of its wicked inhabitants once and for all. Most commentators seem to think that John is rehearsing the trumpet plagues from a different point of view, with the focus of the trumpets being announcements of God's judgments to the world. On the other hand, the description of the plagues from the vials/bowls is the same message directed to the wicked, and worded in a such a way as to be a warning of their final and permanent destruction. [The serious reader will also notice a third rendition or recitation of the destruction of the wicked as being likened to the final harvest and great feast in which the angels harvest the souls of the wicked to be cast into hell (Rev 14:19-20) and the "supper of the great God" (Rev. 19:17-21) where the corpses of the slain will be consumed by the beasts and fowls of the air. (Isaiah 34:3, 11-15)] The vials/bowls are used in John's narration because of their relation to the temple and the altar. The bowls/vials were used in temple worship to perform sacred rites such as burning incense and transporting live embers and coals to the altar and to catch the blood of sacrifices. It is interesting to note that the altar and all that is associated with it is now the focal point, but not of peaceful worship, safety, sanctuary, and personal cleansing. It now becomes the launch site from which the seven angels stand over the earth with the vials/bowls which now contain [literally or symbolically] some deadly agent with which to smite the wicked:

The contents of the first vial are poured upon the earth and a grievous sore appears on man, but only on those who had the mark of the beast and worshipped his image (Rev. 16:2).

The contents of the second vial are poured upon the sea and it turns to blood and it seems as if man is forced to consume the blood of man (Rev. 16:3-4). [Take note of Rev. 17:15 and Jeremiah 51:13 for help in interpreting this verse.] In this context the sea may have the dual meaning of both the literal seas and a spiritually decadent society.

The contents of the third vial are poured upon the earth and the rivers and fountains of water turn to blood (Rev. 16:4-7).

The contents of the fourth vial are poured upon the sun and man is scorched with fire. Man then blasphemes God. Plagues torment man because he will not repent (Rev. 16:8-9).

The contents of the fifth vial are poured upon "the seat of the beast" and his "kingdom" is filled with darkness. The wicked curse God and are covered with sores and filled with pain. (Rev. 16:10-11) (Deut. 28:28-29; Isaiah 13:9-10; 28:14-15; 60:2; D&C 84:49; 112:23) (Rev. 13:1,5-6; 17:3) This is a difficult passage to interpret, because it is not clear whether it speaks of literal or spiritual darkness, and the curse is specifically upon the "seat" of the beast and upon his "kingdom." This is an attack against Satan, his places of power, the anti-Christ, and the 'beast' in his many and varied forms as well as against the people who have relied upon the 'beast' for their livelihood, prosperity and gain. At the same time these verses seem to indicate that the power of God will be with His saints. It is apparent that once the tribulations and judgements start the distinctions between Zion and Babylon, a great divide will grow between Good and Evil, and mortals will be obliged to quickly choose one or the other. There won't be time for straddling or delay. This scenario will create a scene of chaos and confusion without parallel in history.

The contents of the sixth vial are poured upon the river "Euphrates." The land is made dry. Unclean spirits and Satanic darkness cover the earth as the armies of the world prepare for Armageddon (Rev. 16:12-16).

The contents of the seventh vial are poured out into the air, and there is great thundering, hail and lightning followed by catastrophic earthquakes, and finally, the fullness of the fierceness of God's wrath (Rev. 16:17-21). [Note that the seven trumpets sounding and the curses of the seven vials do not correspond with each of the seven seals of the book that is closed with seven seals, only in so far that the pouring of the vials and the sounding of the trumpets begin sometime after the seventh seal is broken.]

VIALS OF ODOURS – (Rev. 5:8; 8:3-4) (Psalms 141:2) Censers/Bowls of burning incense which represent the prayers of the faithful Saints.

VINE – (Rev. 14:18-19) Metaphor for the corrupt societies and nations of the earth. *See* **Clusters of the Vine**.

VIRGINS – (Rev. 14:4) (Jeremiah 18:13; 2 Cor. 11:2) Those who live the law of chastity and marry according to the proper priesthood order; moral cleanliness; The Lord's covenant people have been referred to as "virgins" in the scriptures. Those who remain true to Jesus Christ and in no way commit spiritual adultery. In this regard the **virgins** who surround the heavenly throne and worship God are to be contrasted with those who fornicate with the **harlot Babylon**.

VOICE[S], LOUD/OF THUNDER/GREAT – (Rev. 1:12; 4:5; 5:12; 6:1,10; 7:2,10; 8:5,13; 10:3-4; 11:12,15,19; 12:10; 14:2,7,9,15; 16:17-18; 19:6,17; 21:3) (Joel 3:16; Ezek. 1:24; John 12:29; D&C 43:25; 88:90; 133:22) Declaration or proclamation made so that all might hear. Heavenly voices, including those of God and His Son, have been likened to the noise of thunder.

VOICE AS MANY WATERS – *See* **Waters, Voice as Many**.

- 𝒲 -

WAIT UPON/WAIT FOR THE LORD – *See* **Endure well to the end**.

WALL GREAT AND HIGH – (Rev. 21:12) Symbolic of the peace and security to be found among the inhabitants of the **New Jerusalem**. The city will be surrounded by a great wall that will be built upon the foundation of precious stones and the Twelve Apostles. Its gates, which will be watched over by angels, will be as **pearls** and the names of the tribes of Israel will be inscribed upon the gates.

WAR — (Rev. 17:14; 19:11, 19) State of open and violent conflict and hostility; Struggle between opposing forces in order to achieve a certain end.

WAR IN HEAVEN, PREMORTAL – (Rev. 12:7-12) (Isaiah 14:12-15; Abr. 3:28) The struggle which began in Heaven is in full swing in mortality; In fact, the chronology and placement of these verses in chapter 12 suggest that from now on the conflict between good and evil will actually intensify here on earth before things get better. Satan drew a third of the host of heaven with him (Rev. 12:4), and when they were cast out, they brought with them the knowledge that they had in the spirit world, while our knowledge was temporarily taken from us through our birth into mortality. John's description of this on-going struggle, expressed in very symbolic language, is quite graphic: "The dragon [Satan] was wroth [angry] with the woman [the Church], and went to make war with the remnant of her seed [the saints], which keep the commandments of God, and have the testimony of Jesus Christ" (Rev. 12:17). *See* **Satan, Premortal Existence**.

WARS AND RUMORS OF WARS – (Rev. 9:1-19) (JS-Matthew 1:28; Ezek. 38-39; D&C 45:26) One of the significant signs of the last days is that the people of the earth will be in a constant state of warfare one with another or threatening war one against another.

WASHED IN HIS BLOOD – (Rev. 1:5; 7:14) (3 Nephi 27:19) To repent and be cleansed of sin through the Atonement [sacrifice] and mercy [grace] of the Lord Jesus Christ.

WATER AS A FLOOD – (Rev. 12:15) The **dragon** [Satan] pursues and fights against the **woman** [the Church] and attempts to destroy her with a **flood** of water, or in other words, a **flood** of lies, oppression, persecution and wickedness. *See* **Frogs**.

WATER OF LIFE – (Rev. 7:16-17; 21:6; 22:1,17) (Jeremiah 17:13; Zech. 18:8; John 4:13-14; 6:35; 1 Nephi 11:25; Alma 5:34; D&C 10:66; 63:23) Living water of which we partake and never thirst again due to the refreshing and renewing features of the water; Revelation; Gift of the Holy Ghost; Jesus Christ, Love of God; (Ezek. 47:8-9; Joel 3:18; Zech. 14:8) An additional benefit of the Water of Life is that it will heal the waters that were previously cursed because of the wickedness of man. This healing may be interpreted as being either literal of figurative.

WATERS/OCEAN/SEA, [many waters, overflowing waters] – (Rev. 10:2; 13:1; 17:1,15; 21:1) Societies, institutions, peoples and nations of the earth. The waters represent the source or the origin of the [image of the] first "beast . . . out of the sea." The ocean and seas are traditionally viewed as sources of chaos, trouble and mystery. Often in prophetic language the imagery and symbolism of "overflowing" and "flooding" is associated with plagues that spread throughout the earth and numerous hosts of conquering armies that plunder the peoples of the world.

WATERS TO BE CURSED – (Rev. 8:8-11) (Psalms 78:44; D&C 61:4-5,14) The third part of all things in and on the waters will be destroyed, and the waters will be made to be "bitter;" (Rev. 8:8; 16:3-6) (Ex.

7:14-25) The sea and "fountains of water" are turned as to blood.

WATERS, VOICE AS MANY – (Rev. 1:15; 14:2; 19:6) (Ezek. 43:2; D&C 110:3; 133:22) Expression used to describe the voice of the Lord which emphasizes its qualities of majesty, power and authority. The sound of "**many waters**," such as a rushing river or the waves beating upon the shore, has a tendency also to provide peace and comfort.

WAXED — (Rev. 18:3) Have grown, became.

WEALTH – see **Materialism**.

WEDDING SUPPER OF THE LAMB – *See* **Marriage Feast/Supper of the Lamb**.

WHITE – Color symbolizing purity, righteousness, holiness, great spiritual power.

WHITE CLOUD – (Rev. 14:14) The Lord appears in the midst of a "white cloud" to redeem, or harvest, the saints. The whiteness symbolizes His victory over the world, purity, holiness and grace. In His second coming in glory to reign upon the earth, Jesus will be riding a **white horse** that carries with it the same meaning as above, but additionally the presence of the **white horse** denotes the Lord's triumph and righteous power. The reader will recall that the first horseman of the Apocalypse rode a **white horse**.

WHITE HAIR – *See* **Hair, White**.

WHITE HORSE – (Rev. 6:1; 19:11,14) *See* **Horse**.

WHITE LINEN – (Rev. 15:6; 19:8,14) *See* **White Robes**.

WHITE ROBES/RAIMENT/GARMENTS – (Rev. 3:4-5,18; 4:4; 6:11; 7:9,13-14) (Alma 5:21) Clean and pure clothing worn by the redeemed which symbolizes holiness, priesthood/priestly power and faithfulness to covenants; Clothing worn by those who inherit immortality and eternal life.

WHITE STONE – (Rev. 2:17) Reference to God's acceptance and approval; Precious gift from God given to those who "overcome" (D&C 130:10-11); The **white stone** becomes a Urim and Thummim to the faithful saints that "overcome" the world and receive an inheritance in the celestial kingdom.

WHITE THRONE – (Rev. 20:11) *See* **Throne[s]**.

WHORE – (Rev. 17:1,3,7-18; 19:2) (D&C 29:21) Personified representation which symbolizes and embodies the evil, corruption and abominations of **Babylon**. Synonym for **Harlot**.

WIFE – (Rev. 19:7; 21:9) *See* **Bride**.

WILDERNESS – (Rev. 12:5-6,14; 17:3) Place, situation or condition that is undeveloped, remote, barren, inhospitable; Desolation, abandonment; Narrow places [a wilderness may be a place for discipline, protection, safety, peace, and instruction from God] (Ezek. 34:25; D&C 86:3; 109:73). On the other hand a wilderness is a dangerous place that is out of control, in a state of chaos and without law.

WIND[S] – (Rev. 7:1) (Jeremiah 49:35; Dan. 7:2; 11:4; Zech. 2:6; D&C 133:7) Devastating **winds** are so powerful that they are often viewed as evidence of divine wrath. The "**four winds**" is an expression to indicate the power by which God drives and smites the peoples of the earth as well as expressive of the Lord's power to gather the people to safety from **Babylon** (Mark 13:26-27).

WINE – (Rev. 14:8,10; 16:19; 17:2; 18:3) (Jeremiah

51:7; D&C 35:11) In the same way that one consumes **wine** and becomes intoxicated and senseless, man indulges in the sins and evil practices of **Babylon** and becomes numb to matters of the spirit; (Rev. 14:10) (Job 21:20; Psalms 75:8; Isaiah 49:26; Jeremiah 25:15-17; D&C 88:94) In an ironic twist, the Lord through His prophets has stated that the wicked will eventually be made to drink the "**wine** of [His] wrath." In this case the **wine** symbolically represents both God's righteous anger and the blood of the unrepentant sinner who has refused to seek redemption and be washed clean in the atoning blood of God's Son. *See* **Cup**.

WINE OF HER [BABYLON'S] FORNICATION – (Rev. 17:2,4; 18:3) Idolatry, apostasy, spiritually decadent habits.

WINEPRESS – (Rev. 14:18-20; 19:15) (Isaiah 16:10; 63:3; Jeremiah 25:30; 48:33; Joel 3:13; D&C 76:107; 88:106; 133:50-51) In the scriptural analogy of the Lord having trodden the winepress alone, the implication is that God's purposes will be achieved even if the Lord alone performs them. It was the Lord Jesus Christ who suffered alone in the Garden of Gethsemane and on the cross for the sins and sorrows of this fallen world. No mortal man could ever have the power to redeem himself or another from this mortal condition; **Winepress** is used here as a metaphor for the great battlefields where the wicked gather to slay the wicked.

WINGS – (Rev. 4:8; 12:14) (D&C 77:4) Symbol of power, strength and movement; Symbolic of the power of God's deliverance.

WINGS, SIX – (Rev. 4:8; Isaiah 6:2) The creatures

that surround God's throne have six wings each. The reasoning and symbolic meaning of the wings is clear, however, the meaning behind the number six in this context is not as clear. In a similar vision of God in His temple, Isaiah beheld angelic "seraphims" that had six wings. The number six is generally associated with negative interpretations. Therefore, it is suggested that the creatures possess three pairs of wings. *See* **Three**.

WITHOUT MIXTURE – (Rev. 14:10) (D&C 115:5-6) As in the phrase "wrath of God poured out without mixture," this expression means without mercy, with no let up, without restraint.

WITHOUT THE CITY – (Rev. 14:20) Outside the city, not within the safety of the city walls.

WITNESSES – (Rev. 11:3-12) (D&C 77:15) Two latter-day witnesses in Jerusalem become martyrs for Christ; Synonyms for witnesses are those who bear record, testify, share charity and demonstrate faith through their actions and words (Rev. 19:10; 22:6) no matter the cost; The word "witness" comes from the meaning for the Greek word "martyr." (Rev. 6:9-11; 12:11; 17:6) (Heb. 9:16-17; 11:37-40; 12:1; D&C 135:7)

WOE – (Rev. 8:13; 11:14) (D&C 5:5) Proclamation of deep sorrow, grief, displeasure and/or impending calamity. The angels pronounce three **woes** upon the inhabitants of the earth. John identifies the first two **woes** in Revelation 9:1-21 and 11:14. The third **woe** remains undefined. It begins with the sounding of the seventh trumpet.

WOMAN/MAIDEN – (Rev. 12:1-6) The Church of Jesus Christ [in any dispensation]/the Latter-day

Church of Jesus Christ; Generally speaking, the Kingdom of God and its members/Israel/Zion; City or people of a city [in which case, **woman** is synonymous with the word/symbol **daughter**]; In Revelation 17:1-18 John the Seer is taken into the wilderness a second time and sees a **woman** seated upon a beast, and she is described as a **whore**. Some have speculated that this woman represents an apostate church in the **last days**, however, verse 18 states that this **woman** represents and symbolizes the sins, corruption and wickedness of the city **Babylon**. John makes it clear that throughout the **last days** the **whore/Babylon** will dominate the earth and encompass and surround the Latter-day Saints (Dan. 7:13-27). Hence, the continual and urgent admonitions to flee **Babylon** (Rev. 18:4) (Zech. 2:7; D&C 133:5,7).

WONDER IN HEAVEN – (Rev. 12:1,3) Sign or wondrous event that originates in heaven and is in likeness to things on earth, that is, a shadow or portent of things to occur on earth.

WONDERS/SIGNS OF THE LAST DAYS – (D&C 45:40) *See* **Last days**.

WORD OF GOD – (Rev. 1:9; 19:13; 20:4) (John 1:1; D&C 93:8) Jesus Christ.

WORD OF GOD, POWER OF – (Rev. 1:16) (D&C 33:1; Heb. 4:12) The **Word of God** is an expression with many meanings: Jesus Christ (Rev. 19:13), the scriptures, inspired verbal and written witness or prophecy, and the mortal servants of the Lord. The word and will of the Lord are powerful because the Holy Ghost has the ability to confirm the Truth of the Word to those who diligently seek knowledge and understanding (Alma 17:2-3) and search the scriptures. The Lord personally upholds and qualifies those whom He calls to be his inspired prophets and teachers in mortality and endows them with great power (Num. 11:24-29; Jeremiah 1:7-10; D&C 1:17-20, 37-38). *See* **Spirit of Revelation**.

WORKS – (Rev. 2:26; 3:2) Performances, deeds and ordinances done while in the flesh.

WORKS, ACCORDING TO [HIS] – (Rev. 2:23; 14:13; 20:12; 22:12-13) (James 2:26; Alma 34:34) Man will be judged and rewarded according to the works and deeds he performed while living in mortality.

WORKS OF THEIR HANDS – (Rev. 9:20) Idolatry.

WORLD, END OF – (Rev. 11:15) (JST-Matthew 1:4; D&C 87:6) "The destruction of the wicked" prior to the coming of the Lord in glory. The end of the world as we know it signifies the establishment of the Lord's millennial kingdom.

WORMWOOD – (Rev. 8:11) (Deut. 29:18; Proverbs 5:4; Jeremiah 9:15; 23:15; Lament. 3:15,19; Amos 5:7) *See* **Star Called Wormwood**.

WORSHIP – (Rev. 14:7; 11:16; 15:4; 19:10; 22:8-9) (Ex. 20:2-6; Acts 14:15; D&C 133:39) We are to worship only God, the Father. Worship is an attitude and action of reverence, respect and acknowledgement of God's transcendental holiness and supremacy.

WORTHY – (Rev. 4:11; 5:2; 16:6) Deserving of, qualified for.

WOUND, DEADLY – *See* **Deadly Wound**.

WRATH OF GOD – (Rev. 6:16-17; 14:10-11,19-20; 15:1,7; 16:1,19; 19:11-16) (Isaiah 63:1-6; John 3:36; Rom. 1:18; 2:8; D&C 1:9; 19:20; 20:15-20; 45:3-5; 76:102-107; 87:6; 88:106; 112:24; 133:48-50) An expression of God's fullness of indignation and righteous anger directed collectively at remorseless, unrepentant sinners [**Babylon**] which results in the inevitable demands of justice being executed upon the people of the earth. Jesus Christ, the Son of God, suffered in the flesh for all our sins, pains and sorrows, that we might be healed, saved and not have to suffer the **wrath of God** and the punishing demands of Justice.

WRATH OF THE LAMB – (Rev. 6:16) *See* **Wrath of God**.

WRETCHED – (Rev. 3:17) Afflicted, miserable.

WROTH — (Rev. 12:17) Angry.

ZION – *See* **Mount Sion**.

Bibliography

Conner, Kevin J. *Interpreting The Symbols and Types.* Portland, Oregon: City Bible Publishing, 1980, 185 pp.

Dictionary of Biblical Imagery, Edited by Leland Ryken, James C. Wilhoit, Tremper Longman III, Downers Grove, Illinois: InterVarsity Press, 1998, 1058 pp.

Draper, Richard D. *The Savior's Prophecies.* American Fork, Utah: Covenant Communications, Inc., 2001, 211 pp.

Draper, Richard D. *Opening the Seven Seals.* Salt Lake City, Utah: Deseret Book Company, 1991, 308 pp.

Easley, Kendall H. & Anders, Max. *Holman New Testament Commentary: Revelation.* Nashville, Tennessee: Broadman & Holman Publishers, 1998, 438 pp.

Gaskill, Alonzo L. *The Lost Language of Symbolism.* Salt Lake City, Utah: Deseret Book Company, 2003, 476 pp.

Gileadi, Avraham. *Isaiah Decoded.* Escondido, California: Habraeus Press, 2002, 365 pp.

Gileadi, Avraham. *The Last Days: Types and Shadows From The Bible and The Book of Mormon.* New Edition with Foreward by Hugh Nibley, Orem, Utah: Book of Mormon Foundation, 1998, 292 pp.

Hill, Andrew E. *Guide To Bible Data.* Grand Rapids, Michigan: World Publishing, 1981, 287 pp.

The Life and Teachings of Jesus and His Apostles. Course Manual, Rel. 211-212, Salt Lake City, Utah: Corporation of the President, 1979, 545 pp.

Ludlow, Victor L. *Isaiah: Prophet, Seer, And Poet*. Salt Lake City, Utah: Deseret Book Company, 1982, 578 pp.

Lund, Gerald N. *Selected Writings of Gerald N. Lund*. Salt Lake City, Utah: Deseret Book Company, 1999, 433 pp.

McConkie, Bruce R. *Doctrinal New Testament Commentary, 3 Volumes*. Salt Lake City, Utah: Bookcraft, 1965.

McConkie, Bruce R. *The Millennial Messiah*. Salt Lake City, Utah: Deseret Book Company, 1982, 726 pp.

Millet, Robert L., Editor, *Studies in Scripture, Volume 6: Acts To Revelation*, Salt Lake City, Utah: Deseret Book Company, 1997, 303 pp.

Parry, Donald W & Parry, Jay A. *Understanding The Book of Revelation.*. Salt Lake City, Utah: Deseret Book Company, 1998, 358 pp.

Parry, Donald W & Parry, Jay A. *Understanding The Signs of the Times*. Salt Lake City, Utah: Deseret Book Company, 1999, 556 pp.

Peace, Be Still: Messages of Comfort and Hope in Time of Turmoil. American Fork, Utah: Covenant Communications, Inc., 2003, 107 pp.

Pierce, Darrel L. *The Book of Revelation Unveiled*. Hawkes Publishing, Inc., Salt Lake City, Utah: 1994, 440 pp.

Smith, Mick. *The Book of Revelation: Plain, Pure and Simple*. Salt Lake City, Utah: Bookcraft, Inc., 1998, 306 pp.

The Testimony of John The Beloved: The 27th Annual Sidney B. Sperry Symposium. Salt Lake City, Utah: Deseret Book Company, 1998, 350 pp.

Udall, Marc R. *The Patience of The Saints.* Provo, Utah: Community Press, 1996, 445 pp.

Wilcox, S. Michael. *Finding Personal Meaning in The Book of Revelation: Who Shall Be Able To Stand?* Salt Lake City, Utah: Deseret Book Company, 2003, 338 pp.

Wilson, Walter L. *A Dictionary of Bible Types.* Peabody, Massachusetts: Hendrickson Publisher, Inc., 1999, 470 pp.

Wycliffe Bible Dictionary, Edited by Charles F. Pfeiffer, Howard F. Vos & John Rea, Peabody, Massachusetts: Hendrickson Publishers, Inc., 1975, 1851 pp.

About the Author

Clay A. (Bert) Westover

Bert Westover's immediate family is from the San Diego, California area and Star Valley, Wyoming. He recently took advantage of early retirement from the Federal Government when it was offered and moved with his wife of 30 years to the family home in Fairview, Wyoming. His time is spent doing reading, writing and substitute teaching at the local school district. Most of his teaching days have been spent instructing students in Spanish and English at Star Valley High School. Bro. Westover is on the staff at the Western Wyoming Community College in Afton as a Russian Language instructor.

Brother Westover completed all his primary and secondary education in Southern California. From 1971-1973 he served an LDS mission in Peru. Afterwards He majored in Spanish at the University of Utah, where he took many courses in literature, general linguistics and Russian.

He and his wife, Becky, were married right after the mission in 1973 in the Los Angeles LDS Temple. (She waited.) They have 4 children, a son and three daughters. They also have two granddaughters.

After working 23 years with the Civil Service for the Department of Defense, Brother Westover opted to retire. It was a very rewarding career where he worked on such diverse projects as doing foreign language translation, information management and technical writing.

As for service in the Church, Bert Westover has had many callings. Most of his time has been spent serving in quorum and group leadership positions and in the Sunday School. He was also a seminary teacher for home study. Currently he is in the High Priest Group leadership of the Fairview Ward and is involved in the Afton Wyoming Stake name extraction program.

0 26575 77387 3